Decision Making Under Uncertainty with RISKOptimizer®

A Step-by-Step Guide with Microsoft® Excel® and Palisade's RISKOptimizer Software

Second Edition

Wayne L. Winston
Kelley School of Business
Indiana University

Published by:

Palisade Corporation
798 Cascadilla Street
Ithaca, NY USA 14850

(607) 277-8000
(607) 277-8001 (fax)
http://www.palisade.com (website)
sales@palisade.com (e-mail)

Preface

In our personal and professional lives we are constantly making decisions in an uncertain environment. By combining simulation with an innovative, genetic algorithm based optimization engine RISKOptimizer makes it possible to make the best possible decision given an uncertain environment. I hope the examples in this book will enable RISKOptimizer users to obtain the maximum benefit from this exciting, innovative product.

Acknowledgements

Thanks again to the people at Palisade, particularly Sam McLafferty, Joseph Prisco, Vera Gilliland, Bill Barrett, and Randy Heffernan for their help with this book.

Let me know what you think. I can be reached via email at <u>Winston@Indiana.edu</u> or by phone (812-855-3495)

Wayne Winston
Bloomington, IN
January, 1999

Table of Contents

Chapter 1: Introduction to RISKOptimizer: The Newsperson Problem

@RISK is used to obtain descriptive statistics for situations in which we make decisions under uncertainty. With RISKOptimizer we can actually find the **best** decisions to make under uncertainty. The following easy example will introduce us to the power of RISKOptimizer.

Example 1.1
We need to determine how many Year 2000-nature calendars to order in August 1999. It costs $2.00 to order each calendar and we sell each calendar for $4.50. After January 1, 2000 leftover calendars are returned for $0.75. Our best guess is that the number of calendars demanded is governed by the following probabilities.

Demand	Probability
100	.3
150	.2
200	.3
250	.15
300	.05

How many calendars should we order?

Our final result is in file newsdis.xls. We proceed as follows:

	A	B	C	D	E	F	G
1	Order quantity		200				
2	Quantity demanded		172.5				
3	Sales price		$4.50			Order Quant	Mean Profit
4	Salvage value		$0.75			100	0.3
5	Purchase price		$2.00			150	0.2
6						200	0.3
7	Full price revenue	$776.25				250	0.15
8	Salvage revenue	$20.63				300	0.05
9	Costs	$400.00					
10	Profit	$396.88					
11							
12							
13			Mean = 350				
14							
15							

Step 1: Enter parameter values in C3:C5.

Step 2: In cell C1 we enter a trial value for the number of calendars to order. Later RISKOptimizer will be used to determine the **best** order quantity for calendars.

Step 3: Use @RISK to generate demand according to above probabilities. Type in C2 the formula

   =RiskDiscrete(F5:F9,G5:G9).

This generates a demand for calendars of 100 30% of the time, 150 20% of the time, etc. This demand could also have been generated with the formula

   = RiskDiscrete({100,150,200,250,300},{.3,.2,.3,.15,.05}).

Note in either format the demands are listed first followed by the probabilities. Approximately 30% of the time a demand of 100 will occur, around 20% of the time a demand of 150 will occur, etc.

Step 4: In cell B7 compute Full price revenue with formula

   =C3*MIN(C1,C2).

This ensures that we sell at full-price the minimum of quantity ordered and quantity demanded.

Step 5: In B8 compute salvage revenue with formula

$$=C4*IF(C1>C2,(C1-C2),0).$$

This ensures that number leftover is (number ordered) - (number demanded) (as long as that is >0).

Step 6: In B9 compute ordering costs with formula

$$= C1*C5.$$

Step 7: In cell B10 compute profit with formula

$$= B7 + B8 - B9.$$

Step 8: Our goal is to find the order quantity which maximizes expected profit. At present we ignore the risk associated with our decision. We are now ready to use RISKOptimizer. Basically, RISKOptimizer tries to optimize a (possibly random) function of a **target cell** by changing **adjustable cells**. If desired, the adjustable cells or other spreadsheet cells may have to satisfy desired **constraints.** RISKOptimizer uses genetic algorithms (see Goldberg (1989) and Davis(1991)) to find the "best" values for adjustable cells. The easiest way to explain how RISKOptimizer works is to focus on our current example. We want to maximize the mean profit (this is the target cell) by adjusting the number of calendars ordered (this is the Adjustable cell). It is unreasonable to order more than 300 or less than 0 calendars, so we constrain the number of ordered calendars to be an integer between 0 and 300.

RISKOptimizer now proceeds as follows:

1) For the trial value of adjustable cells in the spreadsheet RISKOptimizer runs enough iterations for the mean profit to satisfactorily converge (you may limit the number of iterations, if desired).

2) Then the mean profit for this order quantity is recorded. RISKOptimizer next selects another order quantity and runs enough iterations to obtain a satisfactory estimate of the mean profit for the 2nd order quantity.

3) RISKOptimizer continues in this fashion to determine mean profit associated with different order quantities.

Genetic algorithm technology is used to operationalize the idea of "survival of the fittest". Thus RISKOptimizer is much more likely to try order quantities with large mean profit than small mean profit. After a while, RISKOptimizer will zero in on the order quantity with the largest mean profit.

RISKOptimizer Settings and Icons

We begin with a brief discussion of the RISKOptimizer icons. These icons are found on the RISKOptimizer ribbon tab (Excel 2007 and later) or toolbar (Excel 2003), which appears in Excel when RISKOptimizer is running.

RISKOptimizer Ribbon Tab

The Model Definition Icon

This icon is used to define the problem you want RISKOptimizer to solve.

A quick summary of the use of the Model Definition icon follows. The best way to understand the use and capabilities of the Model Definition icon is to work through the book's examples.

Target Cell

With RISKOptimizer settings you may choose a target cell for which you maximize or minimize a random function of the target cell. As shown in Figure 1.2 you may maximize the mean of a cell, or minimize the variance or standard deviation of a cell. If you wanted to maximize the 5th percentile of a cell (a typical objective in financial Value at Risk or VAR Models) you would select Percentile (.05). If you want to minimize the probability that a company's profit is less than $1,000,000 you would select Target (1000000).

Figure 1.2

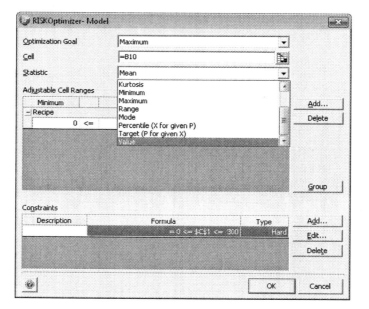

Adjustable Cells

As shown in Figure 1.3, you can next select cells that RISKOptimizer has freedom to adjust. These are called **Adjustable** cells. They can, if desired be assigned lower and upper bounds. You create Adjustable cells by clicking on the "*Add*" button under *Adjustable Cell Ranges*. The "*Delete*" button lets you delete Adjustable cells. RISKOptimizer will attempt to change the adjustable cells to optimize the desired random function of the Target cell.

Figure 1.3

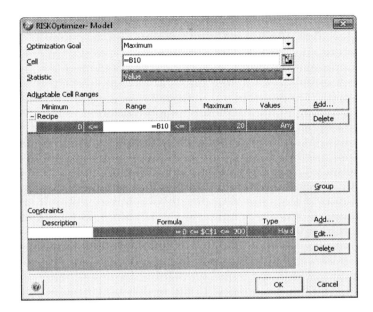

Selecting "*New*" after clicking on the "*Group*" button in Figure 1.3 brings up the Adjustable Cell Group Settings dialog box in Figure 1.4.

Figure 1.4

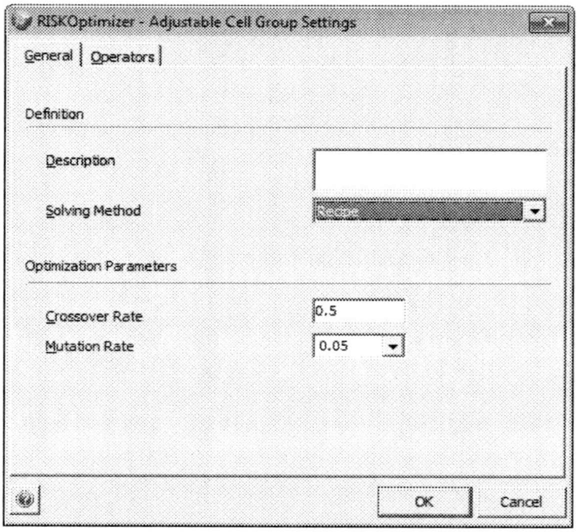

From the Adjustable Cell Group Settings dialog box we select the type of solving method. For most applications, this will be RECIPE. The RECIPE method works like the Excel Solver, but does not take advantage of any special structure your problem may have. We will later give examples of the BUDGET, GROUPING and ORDER methods.

From the Adjustable Cells dialog box we also can select (if desired) lower and upper bounds on Adjustable cells and require Adjustable cells to have (if desired) integer values.

Crossover and Mutation Rates

From the Adjustable Cell Group Settings dialog box we can also modify the **Crossover** and **Mutation** rates. These settings affect the operation of the genetic algorithm used in RISKOptimizer to generate better and better solutions to your problem. As in nature, the genetic algorithm allows good solutions to "breed", but also keeps "less fit" organisms around to maintain diversity in the hopes that maybe a latent "gene" or variable value will prove important to the final solution.

The crossover rate can be set to between 0.01 and 1.0, and reflects the likelihood that future scenarios or "organisms" will contain a mix of information from the previous generation of parent organisms. The mutation rate can be set to between 0.0 and 1.0, and reflects the likelihood that future scenarios will contain some random values. A higher mutation rate simply means that more mutations or random "gene" values will be introduced into the population with each new solution. Because mutation occurs after crossover, setting the mutation rate to 1 (100% random values) will effectively prevent the crossover from having any effect, and RISKOptimizer will generate totally random scenarios.

It helps to understand the functions of these settings by reviewing a full discussion of **genetic algorithms**. See Goldberg and Davis for a discussion of genetic algorithms. Suffice it to say we have obtained best results with Mutations set to Auto and Crossover to .50.

Operators
On the Adjustable Cell Group Settings dialog box you may also select the **Operators** tab. Genetic algorithms use genetic operators to create new members of the population from current members. Two of the types of genetic operators are *mutation* and *crossover* just discussed. As explained, the mutation operator determines if random changes in "genes" (variables) will occur and how they occur. The crossover operator determines how pairs of members in a population swap genes to produce "offspring" that may be better answers than either of their "parents". RISKOptimizer also includes the following specialized genetic operators:

♦ **Linear Operators** – Designed to solve problems where the optimal solution lies on the boundary of the search space defined by the constraints. This mutation and crossover operator pair is well suited for solving linear optimization problems.

♦ **Boundary Mutation** – Designed to quickly optimize variables that affect the result in a monotonic fashion and can be set to the extremes of their range without violating constraints.

♦ **Cauchy Mutation** – Designed to produce small changes in variables most of the time, but can occasionally generate large changes.

♦ **Non-uniform Mutation** – Produces smaller and smaller mutations as more trials are calculated. This allows RISKOptimizer to "fine tune" answers.

♦ **Arithmetic Crossover** – Creates new offspring by arithmetically combining the two parents (as opposed to swapping genes).

♦ **Heuristic Crossover** – Uses values produced by the parents to determine how the offspring is produced. Searches in the most promising direction and provides fine local tuning.

Depending on the type of optimization problem, different combinations of mutation and crossover operators may produce better results than others. Basically, checking every available operator cannot hurt you; it simply increases the arsenal of weapons RISKOptimizer uses to try and find improved solutions.

Constraints   By clicking on the Add button in the Constraints section of the RISKOptimizer Model dialog box we may add constraints on spreadsheet cells. The Constraint Settings dialog box is displayed in Figure 1.5. The Formula option on the Entry Style drop-down menu lets you input a constraint with a formula, such as B10>=D10. We will focus only on **Hard** constraints. A hard constraint **must** be satisfied. As we will see constraints may depend on random functions (such as mean standard deviation, or percentile) of spreadsheet cells. A constraint may be defined as either an **iteration** or **simulation** constraint. An iteration constraint must be satisfied during each iteration of all simulations run by RISKOptimizer. A simulation constraint is checked only at the end of each simulation. Constraints may be entered using simple values or with formulas.

Figure 1.5

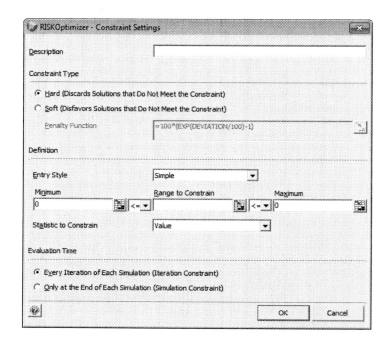

The Settings Icon

Settings

RISKOptimizer Optimization Settings

If you click on the Settings icon you are sent to the dialog box displayed in Figure 1.6.

General Tab

For sampling options we simply select Latin Hypercube as Sampling Type (it is much more accurate than Monte Carlo sampling), and choose Random Values (Monte Carlo) after "When a Simulation is Not Running, Distributions Return." See Figure 1.6. Returning Random Values (Monte Carlo) ensures that when you hit F9 all @RISK functions (and cells depending on them!) will recalculate according to each @RISK function's probability distribution. For instance there will be a 30% chance that demand for calendars is 100, a 20% chance calendar demand is 150, etc.

Figure 1.6

RISKOptimizer - Optimization Settings

General | Runtime | View | Macros

Optimization Parameters

Population Size   50

Random Number Generator Seed   50

Sampling

Sampling Type   Latin Hypercube

☑ Use Same Random Number Generator Seed Each Simulation

When a Simulation is Not Running, Distributions Return

⦿ Random Values (Monte Carlo)

○ Static Values   Expected Values

OK   Cancel

Runtime Tab

Optimization Runtime options tells RISKOptimizer when to terminate its search for an optimal solution. We will usually select *Time*. This tells RISKOptimizer to run for a stated amount of time. If you select *Trials* equal to say, 1000, RISKOptimizer will examine 1000 combinations of Adjustable cells. For *Simulation Runtime* options we will always select *Actual* under *Convergence*. When we choose Actual RISKOptimizer will, for each combination of Adjustable cells examined, run enough simulation iterations to ensure that the random function defined in the target cell and all constraints converge. If this takes too long, then you may limit the number of iterations run for each Adjustable cell combination to, say 1000.

Figure 1.7

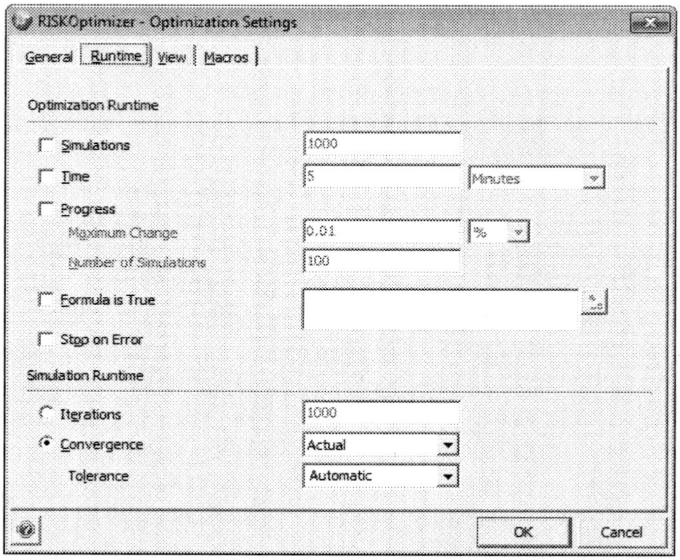

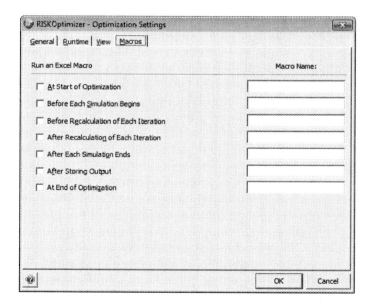

Macros Tab   On this tab, you may run macros at various times during the use of RISKOptimizer. See Figure 1.8. We will give many examples of the use of Macros later in the book.

Figure 1.8

**RISKOptimizer
Progress
Window**

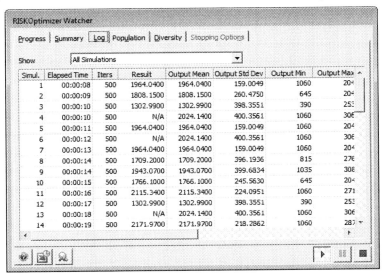

RISKOptimizer Progress	
Iteration:	500 of 500
Simulation:	3
Runtime:	00:00:06 of 00:05:00
Original:	1965.9100
Best:	2159.7800

This window displays during the execution of an optimization. The window contains buttons for starting, pausing and stopping the optimization, and the RISKOptimizer Watcher button.

**RISKOptimizer
Watcher Button**

This button enables us to watch the progress of the optimization or to change our mutation and crossover parameters during a simulation.

The Watcher can show you the results of the simulation run for each trial solution as your optimization is running. You'll see values used for your adjustable cells, the value of the target cell's statistic that you are trying to maximize or minimize and whether your constraints were met (see Figure 1.9). For details on other features of the Watcher button we refer the reader to the RISKOptimizer manual.

Figure 1.9

RISKOptimizer Watcher

Progress | Summary | Log | Population | Diversity | Stopping Options

Show All Simulations

Simul.	Elapsed Time	Iters	Result	Output Mean	Output Std Dev	Output Min	Output Max
1	00:00:08	500	1964.0400	1964.0400	159.0049	1060	204
2	00:00:09	500	1808.1500	1808.1500	260.4750	645	204
3	00:00:10	500	1302.9900	1302.9900	398.3551	390	253
4	00:00:10	500	N/A	2024.1400	400.3561	1060	306
5	00:00:11	500	1964.0400	1964.0400	159.0049	1060	204
6	00:00:12	500	N/A	2024.1400	400.3561	1060	306
7	00:00:13	500	1964.0400	1964.0400	159.0049	1060	204
8	00:00:14	500	1709.2000	1709.2000	396.1936	815	276
9	00:00:14	500	1943.0700	1943.0700	399.6834	1035	308
10	00:00:15	500	1766.1000	1766.1000	245.5630	645	204
11	00:00:16	500	2115.3400	2115.3400	224.0951	1060	271
12	00:00:17	500	1302.9900	1302.9900	398.3551	390	253
13	00:00:18	500	N/A	2024.1400	400.3561	1060	306
14	00:00:19	500	2171.9700	2171.9700	218.2862	1060	287

We are now ready to use RISKOptimizer to determine the calendar order quantity that maximizes expected profit. The relevant RISKOptimizer model definition is given in Figure 1.10.

Figure 1.10

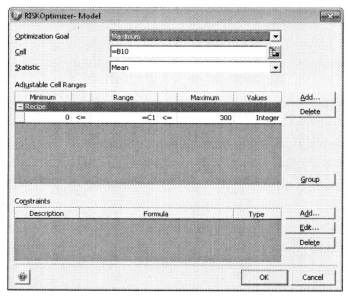

We want to maximize expected profit (the mean of cell B10) by varying the order quantity (cell C1) among the integers between 0 and 300 (inclusive). After running an optimization using the "*Start*" icon, we find that RISKOptimizer selected 200 calendars to maximize expected profit (see Figure 1.1). The expected profit ($350) associated with the optimal order quantity is logged in a comment.

Normal Demand

The assumption of discrete demand is unrealistic. Let's suppose demand is normal with a mean of 200 and standard deviation of 30. To model normal demand simply change cell C2's formula to

$= RiskNormal(200,30)$.

This implies, for example, by the well-known rule of thumb that 68% of the time demand will be between 170 and 230, 95% of the time demand will be between 140 and 260, and 99.7% of the time demand will be between 110 and 290. See file newsnorm.xls.

Let's use RISKOptimizer to determine the order quantity that maximizes expected profit. We will change the allowable range for order quantity to be between 0 and 400 calendars. After a while RISKOptimizer obtains the results in Figure 1.11.

Figure 1.11

	A	B	C	D	E
1	Order quantity		219		
2	Quantity demanded		208.44176		
3	Sales price		$4.50		
4	Salvage value		$0.75		
5	Purchase price		$2.00		
6					
7	Full price revenue	$937.99			
8	Salvage revenue	$7.92			
9	Costs	$438.00			
10	Profit	$507.91			
11					
12					
13			Mean = 459.3899		
14					
15					

RISKOptimizer indicates that ordering 219 calendars optimizes expected profit. The maximum expected profit is $459.39. [1] In reality, expected profit can be shown to be actually maximized by ordering 213 calendars. Should we be disappointed that RISKOptimizer did not find the actual profit-maximizing order quantity? Not really; the expected profit for ordering 219 calendars is within $1 of the expected profit for ordering 213 calendars.

---

[1] Actually, the expected profit indicated by RISKOptimizer is only an estimate of the **true** mean profit. We can use the mean profit found by RISKOptimizer to determine a confidence interval for the true mean profit. See Chapter 26 of Winston (1998) for details.

Managing Risk

With normal demand, the standard deviation of profit when ordering 219 calendars is $88. Suppose we decide the strategy of ordering 219 calendars involves too much risk. Can we use RISKOptimizer to maximize expected profit, subject to a constraint that the standard deviation of our profit does not exceed $50? To accomplish this goal we enter in cell E6 the formula

> =RiskStdDev(B10).

Figure 1.12

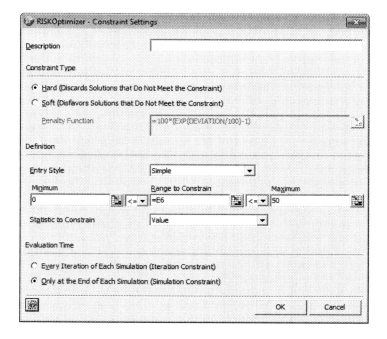

See Figure 1.15 and file newsnorm2.xls for our work. This formula keeps track on each simulation of the standard deviation of profit. We may now incorporate this cell in a constraint. We add the constraint as shown in Figure 1.12 or 1.13.

Our model now look as displayed in Figure 1.14.

Figure 1.13

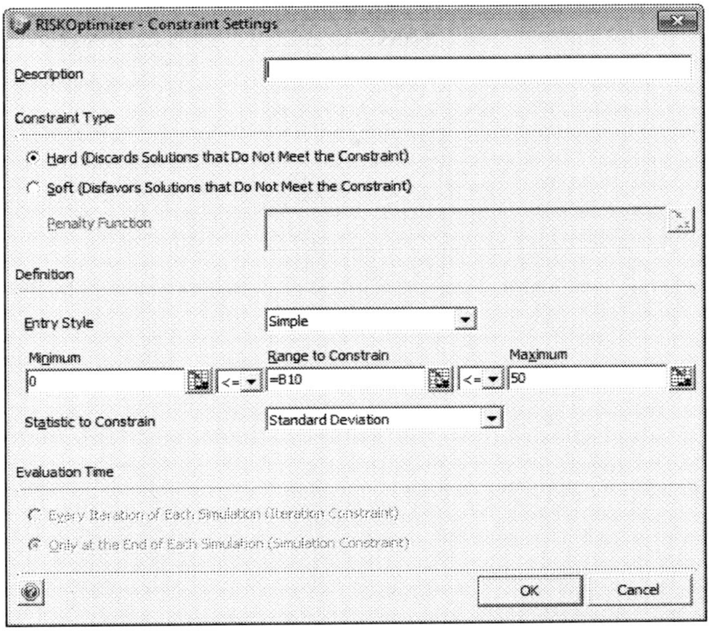

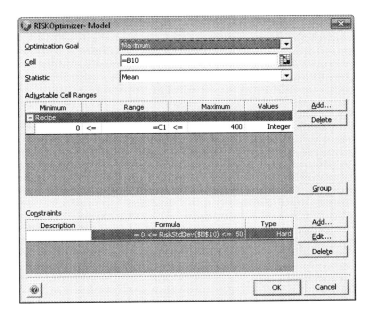

Figure 1.14

After running RISKOptimizer we find the solution given in Figure 1.15.

Figure 1.15

	A	B	C	D	E
1	Order quantity		187		
2	Quantity demanded		200		
3	Sales price		$4.50		
4	Salvage value		$0.75		
5	Purchase price		$2.00		
6				Std dev	48.73
7	Full price revenue	$841.50			
8	Salvage revenue	$0.00			
9	Costs	$374.00			
10	Profit	$467.50			
11					
12					
13				Mean = 442.622	
14					

Thus constraining the standard deviation of profit to at most $50 causes us to reduce our order quantity from 219 calendars to 187. Our expected profit drops from $459 to $443. This is the price we pay for our constraint on risk.

References

Davis, M., *Handbook of Genetic Algorithms,* Van-Nostrand Reinhold, 1991.

Goldberg, D., *Genetic Algorithms in Search Optimization and Machine Learning,* Addison-Wesley, 1989.

Winston, W., Financial Models Using Simulation and Optimization, Palisade Publishing, 1998.

Chapter 2: The Newsperson Problem with Control over Salvage Price

We now modify the newsperson example of Chapter 1 to allow the bookstore owner to sell leftover calendars to customers. The bookstore may also choose the price for leftover calendars. Clearly, we would expect the optimal price charged for leftover calendars to be a **decreasing** function of the number of leftover calendars. The full situation is described in Example 2.1.

Example 2.1

We need to determine how many Year 2000 nature calendars to order in August 1999. It costs $2.00 to order each calendar and we sell each calendar for $4.50. Our best guess is that the number of calendars demanded at full-price is normally distributed with mean 200 and standard deviation of 30.

After January 1, 2000 leftover calendars are sold to customers. The bookstore owner estimates the mean demand for leftover calendars depends on the price for leftover calendars in the following fashion:

	F	G	H
7	**Demand**		
8	Salvage price	Mean Demand	slope
9	0	150	-200
10	0.25	100	-80
11	0.5	80	-120
12	0.75	50	-80
13	1	30	-30
14	1.5	15	

For example, with a salvage price of $0 we could "give away" an average of 150 calendars; with a salvage price of $0.50 we could sell an average of 80 calendars. For prices in between the given values we assume demand varies linearly. For example, if we charge $0.85 mean demand will equal 50 + (.85-.75)*(-80) = 42. Note the "Slope" column gives the slope of the mean demand curve between breakpoints. We assume **actual** demand for leftover calendars follows a normal distribution with a standard deviation equal to 20% of the mean demand. How many calendars should we order and how should the price of leftover calendars depend on the number of leftover calendars?

Solution Our work is in the file newsprice.xls. See Figure 2.1

Figure 2.1

	A	B	C	D	E	F	G	H
1	Order Quantity		217					
2	Quantity Demanded		200					
3	Sales Price		4.5					
4	Salvage price		1.102563					
5	Purchase Price		2					
6								
7	Mean leftover demand		26.9231			**Demand**		
8	actual leftover demand		27			Salvage price	Mean Demand	slope
9						0	150	-200
10	full price sales		200			0.25	100	-80
11	full price revenue		900			0.5	80	-120
12	leftover calendars		17			0.75	50	-80
13	leftover sold		17			1	30	-30
14	leftover revenue		18.74358			1.5	15	
15	total revenue		918.7436					
16	total cost		434			Leftover price		
17	profit		484.7436			Amt. Left	Price	Slope
18						0	1.320510221	-0.012820409
19						25	1	-0.008
20					Mean = 459.71	50	0.8	-0.015476279
21						75	0.413093027	0.007476279
22						100	0.6	-0.002082462
23						125	0.547938446	0.024923261
24						150	1.17101996	
25								

Our Adjustable cells for the problem will include the number of calendars ordered (cell C1) and "price breaks" (G18:G24) which define our pricing policy. G18 gives our price for leftover calendars if 0 are leftover, G19 gives our price for leftover calendars if 25 are leftover, etc. *We assume that if the number of leftover calendars is not a breakpoint, then the price charged is found by linear interpolation.* Thus, for example, if 60 calendars are leftover the price charged is given by .8 + (60 - 50)*(-.015476279) = $0.65. We now describe the spreadsheet setup.

Step by Step **Step 1: In C3 and C5 we enter relevant parameters. In C1 we enter a trial order quantity.** In cell C2 we generate random demand with the formula

$$=ROUND(RiskNormal(200,30),0).$$

Step 2: As in Chapter 1 we compute full-price sales, full-price revenues and leftover calendars in cells C10:C12.

Step 3 : Create the slopes of the mean demand curve in cells H9:H13 by copying the formula

$$=(G10-G9)/(F10-F9)$$

from H9 to H10:H13.

Step 4: **Create the slopes of the price response curve in cells H18:H23 by copying from H18 to H19:H23 the formula**

$=(G19-G18)/(F19-F18)$.

Step 5: **Name the cell range F9:H14 *Lookup* and the cell range F18:H24 *Lookup2*.**

Step 6: **In cell C4 we compute the salvage price charged with the formula**

$=VLOOKUP(C12,Lookup2,2)+VLOOKUP(C12,Lookup2,3)*(C12-VLOOKUP(C12,Lookup2,1))$.

The term VLOOKUP(C12,Lookup2,2) looks up the price corresponding to the largest breakpoint not exceeding the number of calendars actually leftover. The term VLOOKUP(C12,Lookup2,3)*(C12-VLOOKUP(C12,Lookup2,1)) takes the slope of the price response curve in the relevant range and multiplies it by the amount by which actual leftover calendars exceeds the largest breakpoint less than actual leftover calendars.

Step 7: **In cell C7 we use the price computed in Step 6 to determine the mean demand for leftover calendars with the formula**

$=VLOOKUP(C4,Lookup,2)+VLOOKUP(C4,Lookup,3)*(C4-VLOOKUP(C4,Lookup,1))$.

The first term VLOOKUP(C4,Lookup,2) in this formula looks up the mean demand for the highest price break point that does not exceed the actual charged price. The second term in the formula

$VLOOKUP(C4,Lookup,3)*(C4-VLOOKUP(C4,Lookup,1))$

computes the slope of the breakpoint demand curve in the relevant range and multiplies the slope by the amount by which the actual price exceeds the largest price breakpoint less than the actual price.

Step 8: **In cell C8 we compute the actual demand for leftover calendars with the formula**

$= ROUND(RiskNormal(C7,0.2*C7),0)$.

The =ROUND function ensures that demand will be an integer.

Step 9: **In cell C13 we compute the actual number of leftover calendars sold with the formula**

$=MIN(C12,C8)$.

Step 10: **In cell C14 we compute leftover revenue with the formula**.

=C13*C4.

Step 11: **In cell C15 we compute total revenue with the formula**

=C14+C11.

Step 12: **In cell C16 we compute total purchase cost with the formula**

=C5*C1.

Step 13: **In cell C17 we compute total profit with the formula**

=C15-C16.

Step 14: **We are now ready to invoke RISKOptimizer.** Our Model window looks as follows:

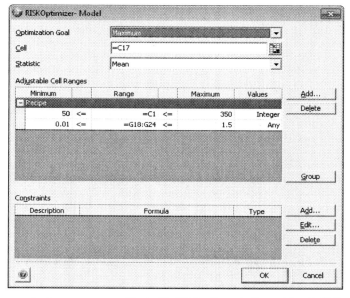

We want to maximize mean profit (cell C17). Our Adjustable Cell Ranges are C1 (order quantity) which we constrain to be an integer between 1 and 350 and price charged for each "breakpoint". These prices are given in cells G18:G24 and are constrained to be between $0.01 and $1.50.

RISKOptimizer tells us that expected profit is maximized by ordering 217 calendars and charging for leftovers based on the following breakpoints:

	F	G	H
17	Amt. Left	Price	Slope
18	0	1.320510221	-0.012820409
19	25	1	-0.008
20	50	0.8	-0.015476279
21	75	0.413093027	0.007476279
22	100	0.6	-0.002082462
23	125	0.547938446	0.024923261
24	150	1.17101996	

Thus if no calendars are leftover charge $1.32; if 25 calendars are leftover charge $1.00, if 50 calendars are leftover charge $0.80, etc. Note that the prices for more than 100 calendars leftover are actually irrelevant, because if 217 calendars are ordered it is highly unlikely that more than 100 calendars are leftover. If, for example, 40 calendars are leftover, then the suggested price for leftover calendars is given by

$$\$1 + (-.008)*(40-25) = \$0.88.$$

Remark

Defining a decision rule by several breakpoints and assuming linear interpolation between them enables the RISKOptimizer user to come up with easily used decision rules for many complicated situations!

Chapter 3: The Multiproduct Newsperson Problem

RISKOptimizer makes it easy to handle newsperson problems in which several products can be ordered. Here is an example.

Example 3.1   Our bookstore is going to spend up to $25,000 ordering four types of calendars. Relevant information on each calendar is as follows:

	A	B	C	D	E	F	G
							Salvage
3	Product	Cost	Price	Worst	Most Likely	Best	value
4	1	$ 3.00	$ 6.00	1800	2000	2500	$ 1.00
5	2	$ 4.00	$ 7.00	1300	1700	3000	$ 1.20
6	3	$ 5.00	$ 7.50	900	1600	1800	$ 1.40
7	4	$ 6.00	$ 8.50	1400	1600	1900	$ 1.60

Calendar 1 costs $3.00 per unit to purchase and sells for $6.00 per unit. The worst case scenario is that customers will want to purchase 1800 of Calendar 1. The most likely scenario is that customers will want to purchase 2000 of Calendar 1. The best case scenario is that customers will want to purchase 2500 of Calendar 1. All units of Calendar 1 that are leftover after New Years Day can be returned for $1.00 per unit. In order to maximize expected profit, how many calendars of each type should be ordered?

Our work is in the file multinews.xls. See Figure 3.1.

Figure 3.1

	A	B	C	D	E	F	G	H	I	J
1	Multiproduct Newsperson Problem				$25,000 to spend					
2				Demand Info						
3	Product	Cost	Price	Worst	Most Likely	Best	Salvage value			
4	1	$ 3.00	$ 6.00	1800	2000	2500	$ 1.00			
5	2	$ 4.00	$ 7.00	1300	1700	3000	$ 1.20			
6	3	$ 5.00	$ 7.50	900	1600	1800	$ 1.40			
7	4	$ 6.00	$ 8.50	1400	1600	1900	$ 1.60			
8										
9	Product	Order Quant	Order Cost	Demand	Sold FP	FP revenue	Sold Discount	Discount Rev	Profit	
10	1	1987	$ 5,961.00	2100	1987	$ 11,922.00	0	$ -	$ 5,961.00	
11	2	1435	$ 5,740.00	2000	1435	$ 10,045.00	0	$ -	$ 4,305.00	
12	3	939	$ 4,695.00	1433	939	$ 7,042.50	0	$ -	$ 2,347.50	
13	4	1434	$ 8,604.00	1633	1434	$ 12,189.00	0	$ -	$ 3,585.00	
14								Total	$ 16,198.50	
15		Total cost	$ 25,000.00							
16			<=							
17			$ 25,000.00						Mean = 16113.6575	
18										
19										

Step 1: In cells B10:B13 we enter trial order quantities for each kind of calendar.

Step 2: In cells C10:C13 we compute the cost of ordering each type of calendar by copying from C10 to C10:C13 the formula

*=B10*B4.*

Step 3: In cells D10:D13 we compute the demand for each type of calendar by copying from D10 to D10:D13 the formula

=ROUND(RiskTriang(D4,E4,F4),0).

Note that the =RiskTriang function generalizes the usual notion of a base case, best case, and worst case scenarios by allowing all cases between the best and worst a chance of occurring.

Step 4: In cells E10:E13 compute the number of each calendar type sold at full price by copying from E10 to E10:E13 the formula

=MIN(D10,B10).

Step 5: In cells F10:F13 compute the full price revenue earned by each calendar by copying from F10 to F11:F13 the formula

=E10*C4.

Step 6: In cells G10:G13 compute the number of each calendar sold at a discount by copying from G10 to G11:G13 the formula

=IF(B10>D10,B10-D10,0).

Step 7: In cells H10:H13 compute discount revenue for each calendar by copying from H10 to H11:H13 the formula

=G10*G4.

Step 8: In cells I10:I13 compute profit earned from each calendar by copying from I10 to I11:I13 the formula

=F10+H10-C10.

Step 9: In I14 compute total profit with the formula

=SUM(I10:I13).

Step 10: In cell C15 compute total amount spent to purchase calendars with the formula

=SUM(C10:C13).

Step 11: We are now ready to use RISKOptimizer to maximize expected profit.
Our Model window is shown below.

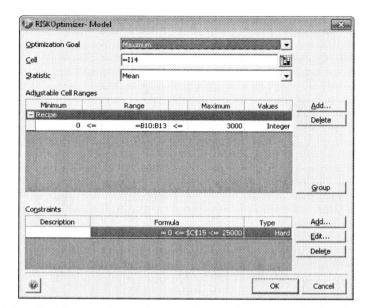

Our Adjustable Cell Ranges (B10:B13) are the number ordered of each calendar. We constrain these to be integers between 1 and 3000. We add the constraint that on each simulation the total order cost (cell C15) is less than or equal to $25,000. By labeling this constraint as a simulation constraint, RISKOptimizer will check it at the end of each simulation.

RISKOptimizer found expected profit to be maximized by the solution given in Figure 3.1:

♦ Order 1987 of Calendar 1, order 1435 of Calendar 2, order 939 of Calendar 3, and order 1434 of Calendar 4.

♦ This strategy incurs ordering costs of $25,000.

♦ The simulation indicates that expected profit equals $16,113.66.

Chapter 4: The Newsperson Problem with Historical Data

In this chapter we show how historical data can be used to model full price and clearance demand for a newsperson problem.

Example 4.1   Sears is trying to determine how many pairs of Levi's slacks to order for the 1997 fashion season. Past demand for Levi's at full price and at clearance price is given in Figure 4.1.

Figure 4.1

	A	B	C	D	E
		Full-price		Clearance	Clearance
3	Year	Demand	Growth	demand	/FP
4	1990	5.00E+05			
5	1991	6.00E+05	1.20E+00	2.00E+05	3.33E-01
6	1992	6.60E+05	1.10E+00	2.80E+05	4.24E-01
7	1993	8.50E+05	1.29E+00	3.00E+05	3.53E-01
8	1994	9.50E+05	1.12E+00	3.00E+05	3.16E-01
9	1995	1.00E+06	1.05E+00	3.60E+05	3.60E-01
10	1996	1.20E+06	1.20E+00	5.00E+05	4.17E-01
11		mean	1.16E+00		3.67E-01
12		sigma	0.08541		0.04415

For most of the season, Levi's sell for $30 a pair. Sears pays $15 per pair of Levi's. At the end of the season leftover Levi's are put up for sale at a clearance price of $18. How many Levi's should Sears order at the beginning of the season?

Solution   Our work is in file levis.xls. See Figures 4.1 and 4.2. The key to this problem is modeling the full price and clearance price demand for Levi's. From Figure 4.1 it seems reasonable to model the year to year percentage growth of full price demand for Levi's as a normal random variable with mean 1.16 and standard deviation of .085. It also seems reasonable to model the clearance demand to be a fraction of full-price demand that is normally distributed with a mean of .367 and standard deviation of .044.

Figure 4.2

	A	B	C	D	E
14					
15	Levi's Ordered	1.73E+06			
16	Full-price demand	1.34E+06			
17	Clearance demand	4.29E+05			
18	Unit cost	$15.00			
19	Full price	$30.00			
20	Clearance price	$18.00			
21	Full-price units sold	1.34E+06			
22	Available for clearance	3.90E+05			
23	Clearance units sold	3.90E+05			
24					
25					
26					
27	Full price revenue	$40,111,679.27			
28	clearance revenue	$7,024,932.44			
29	order cost	$25,909,950.00			
30	profit	$21,226,661.71			
31					
32					
33					Mean = 1.7762E+007
34					
35					

We now proceed as follows:

Step 1: Enter in cell B15 a trial value for the number of Levi's ordered.

Step 2: In cell B16 generate full-price demand for Levi's with the formula

$=B10*RiskNormal(C11,C12).$

This formula embodies the assumption that full-price demand for 1997 will grow by an average of 16% over 1996 with the growth rate having a standard deviation of 8.5%.

Step 3: In cell B17 generate clearance demand with the formula

$=B16*RiskNormal(E11,E12).$

This formula ensures that actual clearance demand (as a fraction of full-price demand) is normally distributed with a mean of 36.7% and a standard deviation of 4.4%.

Step 4: In cells B18-B20 enter the unit cost, full-price and clearance price.

Step 5: In cell B21 compute the number of units sold at full-price with the formula

$=MIN(B15,B16),$

Step 6: In cell B22 compute the number of units available to be sold at clearance with the formula

$=MAX(0,B15-B21).$

Step 7: In cell B23 compute the number of units actually sold at clearance with the formula

$= MIN(B22,B17).$

Step 8: In cell B27 compute full-price revenue with the formula

$=B19*B21.$

Step 9: In cell B28 compute clearance price revenue with the formula

$=B23*B20.$

Step 10: In cell B29 compute ordering cost with the formula

$=B18*B15.$

Step 11: In cell B30 compute profit with the formula

$=B27+B28-B29.$

Step 12: We now use RISKOptimizer to find an order quantity that maximizes expected profit. Our Model window looks as follows:

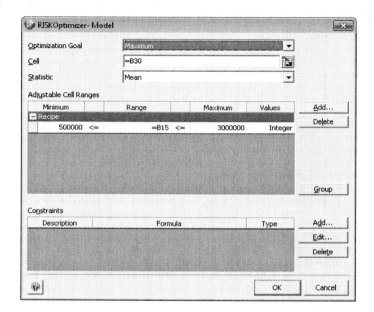

We choose to maximize the mean of cell B30 (profit) by adjusting number of Levi's ordered (cell B15). We constrain the number ordered to be an integer between 500,000 and 3,000,000. From Figure 4.2 we see that RISKOptimizer tells us that ordering 1,730,000 Levi's will maximize mean profit, with mean profit being $17.8 million.

Remark

It is important to note that if we run out of Levi's at full-price or clearance price then sales will not equal actual demand. This causes a lot of difficulty in using historical data to forecast future demand. For example, if in 1991 we ran out of Levi's at the clearance price and we believed we could have sold 50,000 more at the clearance price (if they were available) we should have bumped clearance demand for 1991 up to 250,000.

Controlling both Price and Order Quantity

Suppose Sears may also determine the actual full-price for Levi's. If Sears varies the full-price, they do not know how consumers will respond. Suppose they feel each of the six price response scenarios listed in Figure 4.3 are equally likely.

Figure 4.3

	G	H	I	J	K	L	M
3	Scenario	1	2	3	4	5	6
4	Price						
5	28	0.3	0.2	0.4	0.08	0.04	0.03
6	29	0.1	0.05	0.2	0.05	0.02	0.01
7	30	0	0	0	0	0	0
8	31	-0.2	-0.1	-0.3	-0.2	-0.05	-0.03
9	32	-0.45	-0.3	-0.5	-0.4	-0.1	-0.08

For example, there is a 1/6 chance that Scenario 1 will occur. If Scenario 1 occurs, then a price cut to $28 will increase demand by 30%, etc. Our work for this model is contained in the file leviprice.xls. See Figure 4.4.

Our work is very similar to the previous model. We insert two rows below row 16 and use these rows to generate a price scenario and an actual full-price demand.

Figure 4.4

	A	B	C	D	E
14					
15	Levi's Ordered	1.86E+06			
16	Base Full-price demand	1.40E+06			
17	Price response scenario	6			
18	Actual full-price demand	1411520.388			
19	Clearance demand	502645.0978			
20	Unit cost	$15.00			
21	Full price	$29.00			
22	Clearance price	$18.00			
23	Full-price units sold	1.41E+06			
24	Available for clearance	4.52E+05			
25	Clearance units sold	4.52E+05			
26					
27					
28					
29	Full price revenue	$40,934,091.25			
30	clearance revenue	$8,143,841.02			
31	order cost	$27,959,340.00			
32	profit	$21,118,592.27			
33					
34					
35				Mean = 2.1674E+007	
36					

Step 1: In cell B17 we randomly generate a price response scenario with the formula

=RiskDuniform(H3:M3).

This formula generates integers between 1 and 6, with each number having a 1/6 chance of occurring.

Step 2: In cell B18 we generate the actual full-price demand with the formula

=B16*(1+VLOOKUP(B21,G5:M9,B17+1)).

This formula adjusts the base case demand for $30 by the effect of the chosen price as given in the randomly chosen price response scenario.

Step 3: In B23 we adjust the number of full-price units sold to key off actual demand with the formula

=MIN(B15,B18).

Step 4: We are now ready to use RISKOptimizer to determine the profit maximizing price-order quantity combination. We choose to maximize mean profit (cell B32). We constrain our order quantity (B15) to be an integer between 0 and 3,000,000. We also constrain our price (B21) to be an integer between $28 and $32.

Our RISKOptimizer Model window follows:

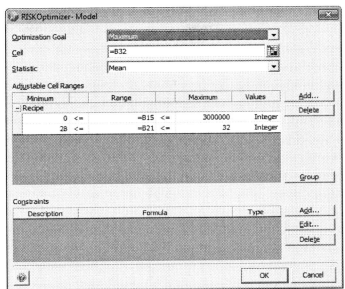

RISKOptimizer recommends that we charge $29 and order 1,860,000 calendars. Mean profit will be $21,674,000.

Chapter 5: The Newspaper Problem with Diversion

Consider a supermarket (Safeco) that stocks Coca-Cola, Pepsi, Diet Coke and Diet Pepsi. The store has a limited amount of shelf space available. In reality, some customers will buy their second choice of soda if their first choice is out of stock. For example, some (but not all) Pepsi drinkers are willing to buy Coca-Cola if Pepsi is out of stock. This phenomenon is known as **diversion**. To make the best possible order decision, Safeco should account for diversion of demand. The following example shows how to model diversion of demand.

Example 5.1   Coca-Cola and Pepsi products are delivered once a week to Safeco. The weekly demand (in six-packs) for Coca-Cola, Pepsi, Diet Coke and Diet Pepsi follows a Poisson random variable with the mean demand for each product given in Figure 5.1. Figure 5.1 also contains the cost per six pack and sales price for each product. Actual weekly demand for each product is computed (see file newsdiv.xls) by copying the formula

$$=RiskPoisson(B4)$$

from C4 to C5:C7. Safeco has enough shelf space to stock up to 950 six-packs of soda.   Assume that each Coke drinker's second choice is Pepsi and each Pepsi drinker's second choice is Coke. Also each Diet Coke drinker's second choice is Diet Pepsi and each Diet Pepsi drinker's second choice is Diet Coke.   Assume that there is a 40% chance that a customer whose first choice is unavailable will purchase her second choice. How many six-packs of each product should Safeco order?

Figure 5.1

	A	B	C	D	E
1	Newsperson with diversion				
2	40% diversion				
3	Demand	Mean	Actual	Cost	Price
4	Coke	280	287	$ 1.50	$ 2.50
5	Pepsi	250	227	$ 1.70	$ 2.40
6	Diet Coke	220	192	$ 1.60	$ 2.50
7	Diet Pepsi	180	191	$ 1.60	$ 2.40

The key to analyzing diversion is to note that for any pair of substitute products there are four cases to consider. To illustrate the four cases, let's focus on Coca-Cola and Pepsi.

1) **Demand for Coca-Cola and Pepsi are both less than or equal to the available stock for each product.** Then sales of each product will equal demand for each product and no diversion occurs.

2) **Demand for Coca-Cola and Pepsi are both greater than the available stock for each product.** Then sales of each product will equal stock for each product and no diversion occurs.

3) **Demand for Coca-Cola exceeds available stock and demand for Pepsi is less than available stock.** Then an average of 40% of all Coca-Cola drinkers who find no Coca-Cola available will try to buy Pepsi.

4) **Demand for Pepsi exceeds available stock and demand for Coca-Cola is less than available stock.** Then an average of 40% of all Pepsi drinkers who find no Pepsi available will try to buy Coca-Cola.

We are now ready to set up the spreadsheet. See Figure 5.2.

Figure 5.2

	A	B	C	D	E	F	G	H	I	J
1	Newsperson with diversion									
2	40% diversion									
3	Demand	Mean	Actual	Cost	Price					
4	Coke	280	302	$ 1.50	$ 2.50					
5	Pepsi	250	258	$ 1.70	$ 2.40					
6	Diet Coke	220	205	$ 1.60	$ 2.50					
7	Diet Pepsi	180	176	$ 1.60	$ 2.40					
8										
9		Ordered	Cost	Sold without diversion	Sold with diversion	Revenue	Profit			
10	Coke	287	$ 430.50	287	0	$ 717.50	$ 287.00			
11	Pepsi	259	$ 440.30	258	1	$ 621.60	$ 181.30			
12	Diet Coke	228	$ 364.80	205	0	$ 512.50	$ 147.70			
13	Diet Pepsi	176	$ 281.60	176	0	$ 422.40	$ 140.80			
14						Total	$ 756.80			
15	Total ordered	950								
16		<=								
17	Shelf space	950							Mean = 732.9405	
18										

Step 1: In B10:B13 we enter trial values for the amount ordered of each product.

Step 2: In C10:C13 we compute the cost of ordering each product by copying from C10 to C11:C13 the formula

 =B10*D4.

Step 3: In D10:D13 we compute the number of six-packs sold (without diversion) of each product. This is simply the minimum of the amount ordered of the product and the demand for the product. In D10 we compute the six-packs of Coca-Cola sold without diversion with the formula

=MIN(C4,B10).

Copying this formula to D11:D13 computes the demand (without diversion) for each product.

Step 4: In E10:E13 we compute the demand (from diversion) for each product. In E10 for instance, the demand from diversion for Coca-Cola is computed with the formula

=IF(AND(C4<B10,C5>B11),MIN(B10-C4,RiskBinomial(C5-B11,0.4)),0).

This formula implies that diversion sales of Coca Cola will occur only if demand for Coca-Cola is less than the quantity of Coca-Cola ordered and the demand for Pepsi exceeds the quantity ordered of Pepsi. The term *RiskBinomial(C5-B11,0.4)* computes the number of Pepsi drinkers who want to buy Coca-Cola. Of course, only B10 - C4 six packs are available for diversion. In a similar fashion, cells E11:E13 compute the sales for diversion for other products.

Product	Cell	Formula to Compute Diversion
Pepsi	E11	=IF(AND(C5<B11,C4>B10),MIN(B11-C5,RiskBinomial(C4-B10,0.4)),0)
Diet Coke	E12	=IF(AND(C6<B12,C7>B13),MIN(B12-C6,RiskBinomial(C7-B13,0.4)),0)
Diet Pepsi	E13	=IF(AND(C7<B13,C6>B12),MIN(B13-C7,RiskBinomial(C6-B12,0.4)),0)

Step 5: In F10:F13 we compute the revenue earned from sales of each product by copying

=SUM(D10:E10)*E4

from F10 to F11:F13.

Step 6: In G10:G13 we compute the profit earned from each product by copying the formula

=F10-C10

from G10:G13. Total profit is computed in G14 with the formula

=SUM(G10:G13).

Step 7: In cell B15 we compute the total number of six-packs ordered with the formula

=SUM(B10:B13)

Step 8: We are now ready to use RISKOptimizer to compute the order quantities that maximize expected profit. Our RISKOptimizer model is given in Figure 5.3.

Figure 5.3

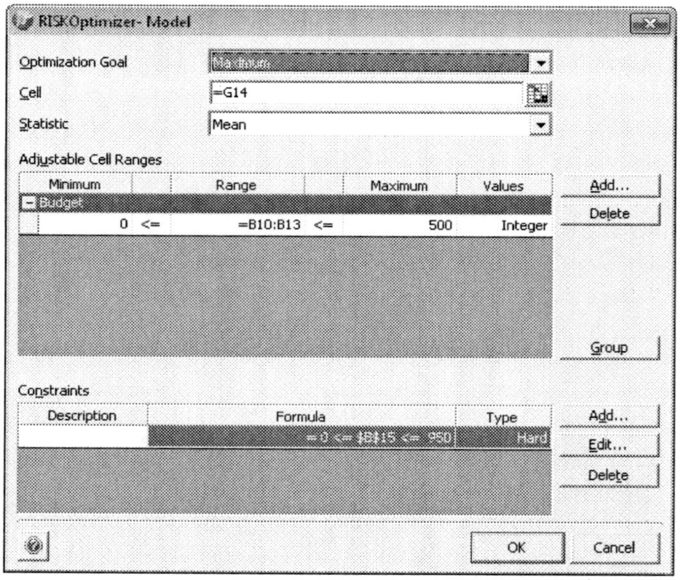

We choose to maximize mean profit (G14) by adjusting the number of six-packs ordered of each product (cells B10:B13). We constrain the number of six-packs of each product ordered to be an integer between 0 and 500 (it seems unlikely that demand for any product will exceed 500). We also add a constraint (to be checked at end of each simulation) to ensure that at most 950 six-packs are purchased.

As indicated in Figure 5.2, RISKOptimizer tells us mean profit is maximized by ordering 287 six-packs of Coca-Cola, 259 six-packs of Pepsi, 228 six-packs of Diet Coke and 176 six-packs of Diet Pepsi. This ordering policy generates a mean profit of $732.94.

Chapter 6: Yield Management

Airlines and hotels have a special type of inventory problem. As soon as a flight leaves, any empty seat becomes worthless. Whenever a day is done, an empty hotel room has lost potential revenue. The practice of optimally managing "inventory" in situations where the unit (an empty seat or room) "instantly" loses value is called **yield management**. RISKOptimizer makes it easy to perform a yield management analysis.

Example 6.1 Northsouth Airlines has a 100-seat flight flying from Indianapolis to Chicago. Northsouth has two seat classifications: discount ($80 fare) and full fare ($125 fare). Northsouth must determine how many seats to reserve for the discount fare. Northsouth must also decide how many seats they are willing to sell at full fare. They cannot sell too many because the airline incurs overbooking costs of $200 for each ticket holder who shows up and cannot find a seat. Northsouth incurs variable costs of $20 for each passenger. From past history Northsouth believes the total number of people who want to buy a ticket for the flight follows a normal distribution with mean 150 and standard deviation of 30. Northsouth also estimates that half of the people who cannot buy a discount ticket will want to buy a full fare ticket. Also tickets are nonrefundable, and on average 95% of ticket holders show up for the flight. How many seats should be reserved for discount fare? How many total reservations should Northsouth take before cutting off ticket sales?

Solution We will let Northsouth's two Adjustable Cell Ranges be the limit on the number of discount fares sold and the limit on the number of full fares sold. Then the total number of tickets Northsouth will try and sell is the sum of these two Adjustable Cell Ranges. If we let the total number of tickets and the number of discount fares Northsouth is willing to sell be Adjustable Cell Ranges, we would have to define another constraint to make sure RISKOptimizer tried values of total numbers of tickets greater than or equal to the number of discount fares (or else the value for full fares would be negative – we would be buying tickets from our customers!). Our work is in Figure 6.1 and file Northsouth.xls.

Figure 6.1

	A	B	C	D
1	Airline			
2	Seats	100		
3	Discount reserved	65		
4	Total ticket cutoff	104		
5	Full-price available	39		
6	Total coming	150		
7			prob	
8	Sold discount	65		
9	Full price candidates	85		
10	Full-price willing to buy	43	0.5	
11	Full-price sold	39		
12	Total showing up	99	0.95	
13				
14			Revenue	
15	Discount	5200	$80.00	
16	Full-price	$4,875.00	$125.00	
17	Costs			
18	Overbooking	0	$200.00	
19	Variable cost	1980	20	
20	Profit	8095		
21				
22				
23			Mean = 7539.3667	
24				
25				

Step 1: In B2 enter number of seats on the flight. In B3 enter a trial number for the limit on discount fares. In B5 enter a trial number for the limit on full fares. In B4 compute the maximum number of reservations that will be taken with the formula

$=B3 + B5.$

Step 2: In cell B6 we generate the total demand for the flight with the formula

$=ROUND(RiskNormal(150,30),0).$

Step 3: Clearly, everybody who wants to buy a ticket will buy a discount fare if it is available. Therefore the number of discount fares sold is computed in B8 with the formula

$=MIN(B3,B6).$

Step 4: Everyone who wanted to be on the flight and could not buy a discount ticket is a candidate to buy a full fare ticket. In B9 we compute the number of people willing to buy a full fare ticket with the formula

$=MAX(B6-B8,0).$

Step 5: In cell B10 we use the fact that an average of half of all people who get shut out of a discount fare will pay full fare. This lets us compute the number of people willing to pay full fare with the formula

$=IF(B9=0,0,RiskBinomial(B9,0.5)).$

Step 6: In cell B11 we compute the number of full fare tickets sold as the minimum of the number of full fares available and the number of people willing to pay full fare.

$=MIN(B10,B5).$

Step 7: In cell B12 we use the fact that an average of 95% of all ticket purchasers show up to compute the number of people showing up for the flight with the formula

$=RiskBinomial(B8+B11,C12).$

Step 8: In cells B15 and B16 we compute our Discount and Full price revenue. In B15 we compute our discount revenue with the formula

$=B8*C15.$

In cell B16 we compute our full price revenue with the formula

$=C16*B11.$

Step 9: Note that each passenger (over 100) who shows up incurs a $200 overbooking cost. In cell B18 we compute our Overbooking cost with the formula

$=IF(B12>B2,(B12-B2)*C18,0).$

Step 10: In cell B19 we compute our variable cost of servicing passengers on flight with the formula

$= MIN(B12,100)*C19.$

Step 11: In cell B20 we compute our profit with the formula

$=SUM(B15:B16)-B18-B19.$

Step 12: We are now ready to use RISKOptimizer to determine the limits for discount and full fares that maximize our expected profit. Our Model window is shown in Figure 6.2.

Figure 6.2

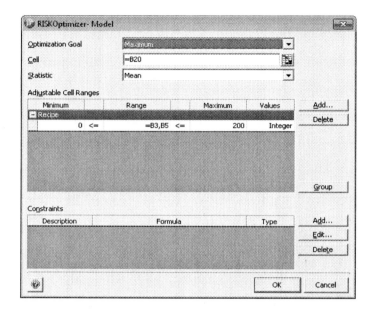

We want to maximize the mean profit (cell B20) by adjusting cells B3 (discount fare limit) and B5 (full-fare limit). We constrain both these limits to be integers between 0 and 200. From Figure 1 we see that RISKOptimizer finds maximum expected profit is $7539. RISKOptimizer recommends that we limit discount fares to 65 and full fares to 39. At most 104 reservations will be taken.

Chapter 7: Optimal Ordering Policies for Style Goods

Retailers such as Sears must determine at the beginning of a season how many to order of fashion goods such as sweaters, dresses, and shoes. The problem is the demand for these products is virtually unknown at the beginning of the season. After a few weeks, however, the retailer has a fairly good idea of what products will be "hits" (or "misses") and can place another order (at a higher cost) for the "hits". The question is how to use the fact that a few weeks of data reduces the variability in our demand forecasts to improve the retailer's profitability. The following example illustrates the basic ideas.

Example 7.1   Sears is trying to decide how many sweaters to order for the current season. An order must be placed now and an order can be shipped (assume instantaneous receipt of all orders) four weeks from now. Sears has collected data on previous forecasts for sweater sales for the first four weeks of the season and actual sweater sales for the season. See Figure 7.1 and file Sears.xls.

Figure 7.1

	A	B	C	D	E	F	G	H	I
2	Forecast Weeks 1-4	Week 1	Week 2	Week 3	Week 4	Rest of season	Weeks 1-4	Actual 1-4/Forecast	Actual/Unbiased Forecast
3	125	38	42	30	23	569	133	1.064	1.1218407
4	310	82	79	76	82	1002	319	1.0290323	1.0849721
5	360	82	77	92	79	1194	330	0.9166667	0.9664981
6	320	78	76	75	70	825	299	0.934375	0.9851691
7	135	42	44	40	39	280	165	1.2222222	1.2886642
8	340	84	86	92	89	1032	351	1.0323529	1.0884733
9	120	18	16	20	20	228	74	0.6166667	0.6501897
10	190	57	59	56	54	746	226	1.1894737	1.2541354
11	230	47	51	44	47	715	189	0.8217391	0.8664102
12	450	88	91	84	86	1052	349	0.7755556	0.817716
13	390	87	82	79	76	881	324	0.8307692	0.8759312
14		Sales price	$ 20.00				mean	0.9484412	1
15		Unit order cost now	$ 9.00				sigma	0.1819379	0.1918283

For example, row 3 indicates that during one season Sears forecasted sales for weeks 1-4 to be 125 and actual sales during those weeks totaled 133. During that season sales after week 4 totaled 569.

It costs $9 per sweater to order now. If an order is placed in four weeks, a fixed ordering cost of $300 is incurred, along with a cost of $10 per sweater ordered. Sweaters are sold for $20.00. At the end of the season sweaters may be sold overseas for $4. Sears buyers have estimated that this season Week 1-4 sales will equal 200. What ordering policy for Sears will maximize their expected profit?

Solution

We will assume that Sears uses an ordering policy of the following form.

♦ Order S sweaters today.

♦ After observing demand for weeks 1-4 determine a forecast for the rest of the season. If the estimated need (N) for sweaters during the rest of the season exceeds a threshold T place an order for M*N sweaters.

We will find that RISKOptimizer chooses S = 872 , T = 110, and M = 1.13. This policy works as follows. Order 872 sweaters now. If after week 4 the estimated need for sweaters is greater than or equal to 110, place an order equal to 1.13 times the estimated need for sweaters.

Step by Step

To begin our analysis, we need to generate actual week 1-4 sales from our forecast.

Step 1: In H3:H13 compute the ratio of actual to forecasted week 1-4 sales for each season by copying from H3 to H4:H13 the formula

=G3/A3.

Step 2: In H14 compute the average of the ratios of actual/forecasted with the formula

=AVERAGE(H3:H13).

We find actual week 1-4 sales averaged 94.8% of forecasted week 1-4 sales. Thus our forecasts were **biased upward**. This is very common!

Step 3: We now determine the ratio of actual week 1-4 sales to an unbiased forecast (obtained by computing .948 times our biased forecast). This is done in cells I3:I13 by copying from I3 to I4:I13 the formula

=G3/($H$14*A3).

Step 4: We compute the mean and standard deviation of Actual/Unbiased Forecasts in cells I14 and I15 with the formulas

=AVERAGE(I3:I13)

and

=STDEV(I3:I13).

We see that we can now model actual week 1-4 sales as a normal random variable with *mean = .948*original forecast* and *standard deviation = .192*(unbiased forecast)*.

We now show how to use actual week 1-4 demand to forecast demand for the rest of the season. We simply run a regression with the dependent variable being rest of season demand and the independent variable being actual week 1-4 demand.

Step 5: Go to the Data ribbon tab, click on Data Analysis, and select Regression. Your dialog box should look as follows:

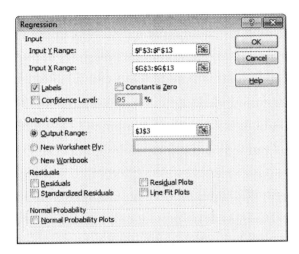

Figure 7.2 displays the results of this regression.

Figure 7.2

	J	K	L	M	N
2					
3	SUMMARY OUTPUT				
4					
5	*Regression Statistics*				
6	Multiple R	0.917979			
7	R Square	0.842685			
8	Adjusted R Squ	0.825206			
9	Standard Error	130.5276			
10	Observations	11			
11					
12	ANOVA				
13		*df*	*SS*	*MS*	*F*
14	Regression	1	821377.8	821377.8	48.2101
15	Residual	9	153337.1	17037.46	
16	Total	10	974714.9		
17					
18		Coefficient	Standard E	t Stat	P-value
19	Intercept	38.24886	113.16	0.338007	0.743109
20	Weeks 1-4	2.937029	0.422999	6.94335	6.73E-05

The p-value of .0000673 indicates that actual week 1-4 demand has a highly significant effect on rest of season demand. The standard error of the regression (in cell K9) of 130 indicates that 68% of our forecasts are accurate with 130.5 sweaters and 95% of our forecasts are accurate with 261 sweaters. Using the results of this regression, **we now model rest of season demand as a normal random variable with mean = regression prediction of 38.25 + 2.94*(actual week 1-4 demand) and standard deviation of 130.5.**

We are now ready to build a spreadsheet that models Sears' ordering policy and the actual demand and sales of sweaters. See Figure 7.3

Step 6: Enter cost parameters in C14:C18 and our Week 1-4 forecast in C19.

Step 7: In cells C26:C28 enter trial values for S, T, and M.

Figure 7.3

	B	C	D	E	F
14	Sales price	$ 20.00			
15	Unit order cost now	$ 9.00			
16	Unit order cost later	$ 10.00			
17	Fixed Cost of later production run	$ 300.00			
18	Leftover price	$ 4.00			
19	Week 1-4 Forecast	200			
20	Week 1-4 actual	211.402022			
21	Rest of season forecast	659.771945			
22	Rest of season actual	424.25204			
23	On Hand at end of week 4	660.597978			
24	Estimated need	0			
25	**Decisions**				
26	Current Order	872			
27	Cutoff on Future Order	110			
28	Multiple for future order	1.13439524			
29	Actual Future Order	0			
30					
31	**Revenues**				
32	Full-price Unit Sales Weeks 1-4	211.402022			
33	Full-price Unit Sales Rest of season	424.25204			
34	Leftover Unit sales	236.345938			
35	Full-price revenue	$ 12,713.08			
36	Leftover revenue	$ 945.38			
37	Total revenue	$ 13,658.46			
38	**Costs**				
39	Original cost	$ 7,848.00			
40	Fixed cost of second order	$ -			
41	Cost of second order items	$ -			
42	Total cost	$ 7,848.00			
43					
44	**Profit**	$ 5,810.46			
45					
46					
47				Mean = 7782.6363	
48					

Step 8: In cell C20 generate an actual week 1-4 demand with the formula

$=RiskNormal(H14*C19,I15*(H14*C19)).$

This formula creates an unbiased forecast and builds in the forecast error found from our past forecasts.

Step 9: In cell C21 we use our regression to compute a forecast for rest of season sales with the formula

$=38.25+2.94*C20.$

Step 10: In cell C22 use the standard error of the regression to compute *actual* rest of season sales with the formula

$=RiskNormal(C21,130.5).$

Step 11: In cell C23 compute how many sweaters from original order are left at end of week 4 with the formula

$=MAX(C26-C20,0).$

Step 12: In cell C24 compute our estimated need for sweaters during the rest of the season with the formula

$=MAX(C21-C23,0).$

Step 13: In cell C29 we compute the size of our future order. Note that we only order if estimated need exceeds threshold T. If an order is placed we order a multiple M of estimated need.

$=IF(C24>=C27,(C24)*C28,0).$

Step 14: In cell C32 we compute our actual sales during weeks 1-4 as minimum of original order quantity and original order.

$=MIN(C20,C26).$

Step 15: In cell C33 we compute our actual sales for rest of season as minimum of sweaters available and actual demand.

$=MIN(C23+C29,C22).$

Step 16: In cell C34 we compute sweaters leftover as *(sweaters available for rest of season - sweaters sold during rest of season).*

=C23+C29-C33.

Step 17: In cell C35 compute full-price revenue with the formula

=C14*SUM(C32:C33).

Step 18: In cell C36 compute discount revenue with the formula

=C18*C34.

Step 19: In cell C37 compute total revenue with the formula

=SUM(C35:C36).

Step 20: In cell C39 we compute the cost of the original order with the formula

=C15*C26.

Step 21: In cell C40 we compute the fixed cost (if any) from our second order with the formula

=IF(C29>0,C17,0).

Step 22: In cell C41 we compute the variable cost (if any) from our second order with the formula

=C29*C16.

Step 23: In cell C42 we compute total cost with the formula

=SUM(C39:C41).

Step 24: In cell C44 we compute profit with the formula

=C37-C42.

Step 25: We are now ready to invoke RISKOptimizer. Our Model window looks as follows:

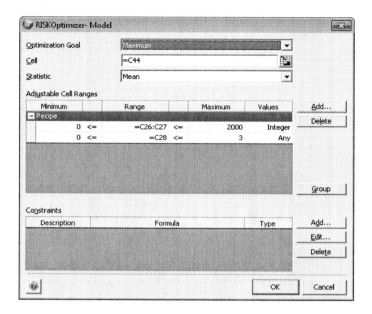

We choose to maximize mean profit (C44). Our adjustable cells are the original order size (C26), the need threshold for a reorder (C27), and the multiple of need ordered (C28). It seemed unreasonable to order more than 3000 sweaters so we limited the number of sweaters on each order to be at most 3000. It also seemed unreasonable to order more than 3 times the number of sweaters needed, so we restricted the multiplier to be at most 3.

From Figure 7.3 RISKOptimizer recommended ordering 872 sweaters now. After observing weeks 1-4 demand we reorder if we estimate that 110 or more are needed for rest of season. We order 13% more than we think we need.

Chapter 8: The Product Mix Problem

Virtually every management science book begins the study of linear programming with the classical product mix problem. The object is to determine a mix of products to produce that maximizes profit subject to limited resources and known demand for each product. The problem with this setup is, of course, that many parameters of the problem are not known with certainty. Of course, demand is always unknown. The amount of each resource used by a product may be unknown. The price of each product may even be unknown. Despite this uncertainty companies must determine what to produce. RISKOptimizer lets us determine a production schedule that is "best" (maximizes expected profit in the presence of multiple sources of uncertainty). In this section we use RISKOptimizer to optimize the product mix in the face of uncertainty.

Example 8.1   Drugco produces four drugs. Each drug uses the amount of raw material, labor, and machine time given in Figure 8.1. For example, Drug 1 uses 4 units of raw material, 3 units of labor, and 2 units of machine time. The sales price of each drug is also given. Demand for each drug is unknown, but best case, worst case and most likely demand for each product is also given in Figure 8.1. During the current month 8000 units of raw material, 10,000 units of labor and 14,000 units of machine time are available. How can we schedule this month's production to maximize expected profit? The drugs will spoil at the end of the month, so leftover units of each drug have no value.

Solution   Our work is in the file prodmix.xls. See Figure 8.1.

Step by Step   We proceed as follows:

Step 1: In cells B4:E4 we enter trial values for the number of units produced of each drug.

Step 2: In cells B10:E10 we compute the actual demand (assuming a triangular distribution) for each drug. We copy the demand for Drug 1 which is computed in cell B10 with the formula

=RiskTriang(B11,B12,B13)

from cell B10 to C10:E10.

Figure 8.1

	A	B	C	D	E	F	G	H	I
1	Product Mix					Revenues			
2							$ 23,125.67		
3		Product 1	Product 2	Product 3	Product 4				
4	Produced	303	1541	774	205				
5	Units Sold	303	943.0077	715.322	205	Mean = 24664.7232			
6	Sales price	$ 14.00	$ 12.00	$ 8.00	$ 9.00				
7	RM	4	3	2	3		Available		
8	Labor	3	3	2	1	RM	8000		
9	Machine Time	2	3	1	2	Labor	10000		
10	Actual Demand	1259.804	943.0077	715.322	481.9714	Machine Time	14000		
11	Worst	1200	900	300	0				
12	Most Likely	1400	1000	800	600		Used		Available
13	Best	1800	1400	1000	1600	RM	7998	<=	8000
14						Labor	7285	<=	10000
15						Machine Time	6413	<=	14000

Step 3: In cells B5:E5 we compute the number sold of each product by copying from B5 to C5:E5 the formula

=MIN(B4,B10).

Step 4: In cell G2 we compute our total revenue with the formula

=SUMPRODUCT(B5:E5,B6:E6).

Step 5: In cells G13:G15 we compute the usage of each resource. In G13 we compute the usage of raw material with the formula

=SUMPRODUCT($B$4:$E$4,B7:E7).

Copying this formula to G14:G15 computes the usage of labor and machine time.

Step 6: We are now ready to use RISKOptimizer to determine a product mix that maximizes expected profit. Figure 8.2 displays our RISKOptimizer Model window.

Our goal is to maximize expected profit (G2). Our Adjustable Cell Ranges are the number of units produced of each drug (cells B4:E4). We add the constraints G13<=I13, G14<=I14, and G15<=I15 as constraints to be satisfied at the end of each simulation. This ensures that we do not use more of any resource than we have available.

Figure 8.2

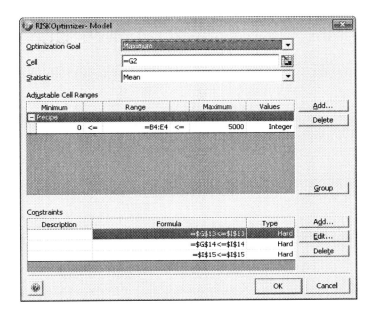

From Figure 8.1, RISKOptimizer indicates that the maximum expected profit we can obtain is $24,665. We should plan on producing 303 units of Drug 1, 1541 units of Drug 2, 774 units of Drug 3, and 205 units of Drug 4.

What If Resource Usage is Uncertain?

Let's suppose that we do not know exactly how much of each resource will be needed to produce the drugs. More specifically, let's assume that the usage per unit produced of each drug is normally distributed and has a standard deviation of .3. For example, this would imply that the amount of labor used per unit of Drug 1 produced would be normally distributed with a mean of 3 and standard deviation of .3. Now let's suppose we want to have only a 5% chance of running short of *any* resource during the month. How can we maximize expected profit? Our work is in file prodmix2.xls. See Figure 8.3.

Figure 8.3

	A	B	C	D	E	F	G	H	I
1	Product Mix					Revenues			
2							$26,041.00		
3		Product 1	Product 2	Product 3	Product 4				
4	Produced	646	529	412	817				
5	Units Sold	646	529	412	817				
6	Sales price	$ 14.00	$ 12.00	$ 8.00	$ 9.00			Mean = 24477.2109	
7	RM	4.205199	3.102702	1.997795	3.381408		Available		
8	Labor	2.908318	3.293896	3.380615	0.835023	RM	8000		
9	Machine Time	1.820009	2.372704	0.981585	2.392784	Labor	10000		
10	Actual Demand	1347.803	1200.599	434.4585	1204.438	Machine Time	14000		
11	Worst	1200	900	300	0				
12	Most Likely	1400	1000	800	600		Used	Shortage?	Available
13	Best	1800	1400	1000	1600	RM	7943.58884	0	8000
14						Labor	5696.27183	0	10000
15						Machine Time	4790.20371	0	14000
16							Shortage	0	
17							Mean Short	0.05	
18								<=	
19								0.05	

We modify our previous formulation as follows:

Step by Step **Step 1: In B7:E9 insert RiskNormal formulas to ensure that resource usage is random.** For example, the formula

> $=RiskNormal(4,0.3)$

in cell B7 ensures that raw material usage per unit of Drug 1 produced is normal with mean 4 and standard deviation of .3.

Step 2: In H13:H15 determine if a shortage occurs for each resource by copying from H13 to H14:H15 the formula

> $=IF(G13>I13,1,0)$.

A "1" indicates we have used more of the resource than is available.

Step 3: **In cell H16 determine if any shortage has occurred with the formula**

=MAX(H13:H15).

A "1" in this cell indicates that a shortage has occurred.

Step 4: **In cell H17 compute the fraction of all iterations of a simulation that yield a shortage with the formula**

=RiskMean(H16).

Step 5: **We are now ready to use RISKOptimizer.** The Model window is shown in Figure 8.4.

Figure 8.4

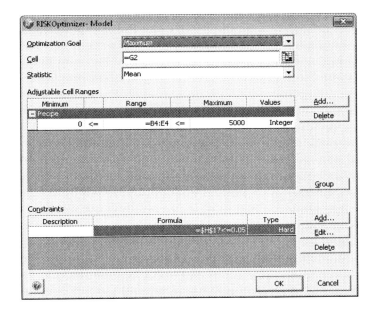

We choose to maximize mean profit (G2) by adjusting the production of each drug (B4:E4). We constrain production of each drug to be an integer between 0 and 5000. To ensure that the probability of a shortage for *any* resource does not exceed 5% we add the (simulation) constraint H17<=.05.

As shown in Figure 3, RISKOptimizer finds maximum expected profit of $24,477 is obtained by producing 646 units of Drug 1, 529 units of Drug 2, 412 units of Drug 3, and 817 units of Drug 4. Note that introducing the uncertainty in resource usage has slightly reduced our profit. If we wanted to be, say 99.9% sure that we did not run out of any resource, we would suffer a much greater profit reduction.

Chapter 9: Agricultural Planning under Uncertainty

At the beginning of each season farmers must determine how to utilize their land. The weather is highly uncertain and one strategy might be best for a dry season and another strategy may be best for a wet season. In the presence of uncertainty about climate, how can a farmer determine a land utilization strategy that maximizes her expected profit?

Example 9.1
Farmer Jones owns a 100-acre farm on which she plants corn, wheat and soybeans and raises cattle. The per acre yield on each crop depends on whether rainfall is dry, medium, or wet. The yield per acre (in bushels per acre) is given in Figure 9.1 (see file Farmer.xls).

Figure 9.1

	A	B	C	D	E	F	G	H	I
1	Farmer Jones			Weather	2.1				
2	Code	1	2	3					
3	Probability	0.2	0.5	0.3					
4	Bushels/acre	Dry	Medium	Wet	Labor	Profit/bushel	Acres	Bushels made	Bushels sold
5	Corn	70	170	80	50	$ 4.00	43.508	7396.3432	4351.197
6	Wheat	80	160	100	60	$ 5.00	45.096	7215.3914	7215.391
7	Soybeans	100	120	90	35	$ 3.00	1.2454	149.44991	149.4499
8		Corn/cow	Profit/cow	Labor/cow	Cows/acre				
9	Cows	30	$ 400.00	50	10		10.15		
10									
11			Profit						
12			$ 94,532.04	◄	Mean = 78637.6315				
13									
14		Used		Available					
15	Labor	10000	<=	10000					
16		Made		Corn fed to Cows					
17	Corn	7396.343	>=	3045.145908					
18									
19				TRUE					

Figure 9.1 also gives the per acre labor requirement for each crop. Each cow requires 1/10 acre of land, 30 bushels of corn and 50 hours of labor. Each cow contributes $400 of profit. It is estimated that there is a 20% chance of a dry season, a 50% chance of a medium season, and a 30% chance of a wet season. Farmer Jones has 10,000 hours of labor available. How can Farmer Jones maximize his expected profit?

We proceed as follows:

Step 1: In G5:G7 we enter trial values for the number of acres assigned to each crop. In G9 we enter a trial value for the number of acres assigned to cows. For reasons that will become apparent later, make sure that a total of 100 acres is used by your trial solution.

Step 2: In cell E1 we generate the type of weather (1= dry, 2 = medium, 3 = wet) with the formula

=RiskDiscrete(B2:D2,B3:D3).

Step 3: In cells H5:H7 we compute the number of bushels of each crop produced by copying from H5 to H6:H7 (and changing the 4 to a 5 in H6 and the 4 to a 6 in H7) the formula

=G5*HLOOKUP($E$1,$B$2:$E$7,4).

Step 4: In cell D17 we compute the corn fed to cows with the formula

=E9*B9*G9.

Step 5: In cells I5:I7 we compute the number of bushels sold of each product. After subtracting off corn fed to cows we compute the number of bushels of corn sold in cell I5 with the formula

=H5-D17.

In cells I6:I7 we compute the bushels of wheat and soybeans sold by copying the formula

=H6

from I6 to I7.

Step 6: In cell C12 we compute our profit with the formula

=C9*E9*G9+SUMPRODUCT(F5:F7,I5:I7).

Step 7: In cell B15 we compute our total labor usage with the formula

=SUMPRODUCT(E5:E7,G5:G7)+E9*D9*G9.

Step 8: **In cell B17 we recomputed the amount of corn produced**. This will allow us to constrain corn produced to exceed corn needed for cows.

Step 9: **In cell D19 we enter the logical formula**

=B17>=D17.

This cell will contain a TRUE if we produce enough corn to feed the cows and a FALSE otherwise. By making D19 an iteration constraint we ensure that we will always have enough corn to feed the cows.

Step 10: **We are now ready to invoke RISKOptimizer**. Figure 9.2 shows the RISKOptimizer Model window.

Figure 9.2

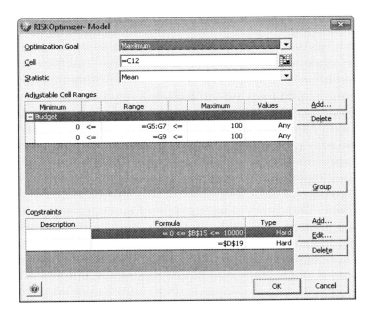

Our goal is to maximize mean revenue (C12) by choosing the number of acres devoted to cows and each crop (G9 and G5:G7) Constrain each Adjustable cell to be between 0 and 100. We select the *budget* solution method. Using the Budget method ensures that on each simulation the Adjustable Cell Ranges will always add to their initial sum (100). This ensures that all simulations use all available land. The constraint B15<=10,000 is a simulation constraint which ensures that each land allocation uses at most 10,000 labor hours. The constraint D19 is an iteration constraint that ensures on each iteration of any simulation that we have enough corn to feed the cows. We enter this constraint by choosing **Add,** choosing Formula in the Entry Style drop-down menu, and typing =D19 in the Constraint Formula field.

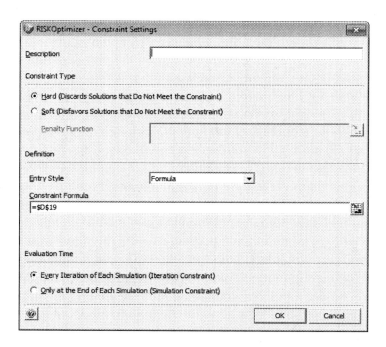

RISKOptimizer reports a maximum expected profit of $78,637. To obtain this maximum expected profit we plant 43.51 acres of corn, 45.10 acres of wheat, 1.25 acres of soybeans, and devote 10.15 acres to cows. Note that even during a dry season we have enough corn to feed the cows. Soybeans, while not very profitable, are utilized because of their low labor requirement.

Chapter 10: Production Scheduling

Most companies need to determine a production schedule in the face of uncertain demand. RISKOptimizer makes it a snap to plan a production schedule that minimizes expected costs in the face of uncertain demand.

Example 10.1   Shoeco needs to plan its production schedule for the next 6 months. They are limited to producing at most 900 pairs of shoes each month with regular time labor and at most 200 pairs of shoes each month with overtime labor. Shoeco incurs the following types of costs:

	A	B
2	var cost rt prod	$12.00
3	var cost ot prod	$20.00
4	holding cost	$0.50
5	shortage cost	$15.00

Thus at the end of each month it costs $0.50 to hold a pair of shoes in inventory and if we fail to meet a unit of demand, a penalty cost of $15 is incurred during each month for which a shortage occurs. At the beginning of Month 1, Shoeco has 400 pairs of shoes in inventory. Shoeco would like to ensure that by the end of the six-month planning horizon, there is at most a 10% chance of a negative inventory position. Demand is normally distributed each month with the monthly mean and standard deviation given in rows 9 and 10 of Figure 10.1. Determine Shoeco's optimal production schedule.

In a straightforward fashion we will keep track of (for each month) beginning inventory, ending inventory, production, and all costs. We will also keep track of the chance of a shortage occurring at the end of month 6. Our work is in the file production.xls and Figure 10.1.

Figure 10.1

	A	B	C	D	E	F	G
7							
8	Month	1	2	3	4	5	6
9	Mean demand	1000	600	800	1400	350	900
10	sigma demand	300	150	150	400	75	250
11	actual demand	1142.789762	770.715998	707.9105311	1288.344609	384.4925806	1372.67723
12	beginning inventor	400	157.2102382	486.4942402	678.583709	290.2390996	656.746519
13	rt prod	900	900	900	900	751	867
14	ot prod	0	200	0	0	0	0
15	ending inventory	157.2102382	486.4942402	678.583709	290.2390996	656.746519	151.069288
16							
17	**Costs**						
18	rt prod	$ 10,800.00	$ 10,800.00	$ 10,800.00	$ 10,800.00	$ 9,012.00	$10,404.00
19	ot prod	$ -	$ 4,000.00	$ -	$ -	$ -	$ -
20	holding	78.60511909	243.2471201	339.2918545	145.1195498	328.3732595	75.534644
21	shortage	0	0	0	0	0	0
22	total	$ 10,878.61	$ 15,043.25	$ 11,139.29	$ 10,945.12	$ 9,340.37	$10,479.53
23		Month 6 Shortage?					
24		0					
25	Prob Mo 6 short	0.1 <=		0.1			
26							
27	Total Cost	$ 67,826.17					
28							
29							
30				Mean = 70747.5725			
31							

Step 1: In cells B2:B5 enter the relevant costs.

Step 2: In B11:G11 we generate the actual monthly demands by copying from B11 to C11:G11 the formula

$=RiskTnormal(B9,B10,0,10000).$

The use of the truncated normal avoids the possibility of negative demand.

Step 3: In rows 13 and 14 we enter trial values for regular time and overtime production.

Step 4: In cell B12 enter our beginning Month 1 inventory of 400 shoes. Compute the ending Month 1 inventory in cell B15 with the formula

$=B12+B13+B14-B11.$

Copying this formula to cells C15:G15 computes ending inventory for each month.

Step 5: **Compute beginning inventory for Months 2-6 by copying from C12 to D12:G12 the formula**

=B15.

Step 6: **In B18:G18 we compute each month's regular time production costs by copying from B18 to C18:G18 the formula**

=$B$2*B13.

Step 7: **In B19:G19 we compute each month's overtime production costs by copying from B19 to C19:G19 the formula**

=$B$3*B14.

Step 8: **In B20:G20 compute each month's holding cost by copying from B20 to C20:G20 the formula**

=IF(B15>0,$B$4*B15,0).

This yields 0 if ending inventory is negative. Otherwise ending inventory is multiplied by the unit holding cost.

Step 9: **In B21:G21 compute each month's shortage cost by copying from B21 to C21:G21 the formula**

=IF(B15<0,-B15*$B$5,0).

If ending inventory is non-negative, the shortage cost is 0. Otherwise we obtain the shortage cost by multiplying the magnitude of the ending inventory by the shortage cost.

Step 10: **In B22:G22 use the summation icon to compute the total cost for each month.** Just select B22:G22 and click on the summation icon.

Step 11: **In B27 compute the total cost for the six months with the formula**

=SUM(B22:G22).

Step 12: **In B24 we determine if a shortage occurred during Month 6 with the formula**

=IF(G15<0,1,0).

Step 13: In cell B27 we determine total cost with the formula

=SUM(B22:G22).

Step 14: We are now ready to use RISKOptimizer to determine a production schedule which yields negative inventory for Month 6 at most 10% of the time and minimizes expected cost. Our RISKOptimizer Model window follows:

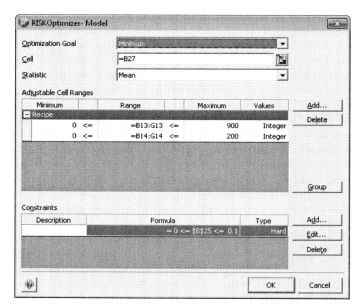

We choose to minimize mean cost (B27) by adjusting regular time production (B13:G13) and overtime production (B14:G14). Each month's regular time production must be an integer between 0 and 900 while each month's overtime production must be an integer between 0 and 200. Our last constraint ensures that each production schedule considered by RISKOptimizer will have at most a 10% chance of a Month 6 shortage. As shown in Figure 10.1 minimum expected cost is $70,748. The optimal production schedule is shown below:

	A	B	C	D	E	F	G
13	rt prod	900	900	900	900	751	867
14	ot prod	0	200	0	0	0	0

Chapter 11: Manpower Scheduling Under Uncertainty

Banks, retailers, phone companies, fast-food restaurants and many other organizations must schedule a workforce in the face of uncertain manpower requirements. RISKOptimizer makes it easy to determine a schedule that can handle the uncertain demand that we face in today's unpredictable world.

Example 11.1   The Smallville Post office does not know for certain how many employees will be needed each day of the week but they believe the number of employees needed each day follows a Poisson random variable with the means given in row 13 of Figure 11.1 (see file post.xls). Employees work five consecutive days. Determine the minimum number of employees needed to ensure that there is less than a 10% chance that a shortage of employees will occur during the week.

Figure 11.1

	E	F	G	H	I	J	K	L
2		32	Work Matrix					
3	Started		Sunday	Monday	Tuesday	Wednesda	Thursday	Friday	Saturday
4	13	1	1	1	1	1	0	0
5	3		Value = 32	1	1	1	1	1	0
6	3		0	1	1	1	1	1
7	0	1	0	0	1	1	1	1
8	7	1	1	0	0	1	1	1
9	4	1	1	1	0	0	1	1
10	2	1	1	1	1	0	0	1
11	Working	26	29	25	21	26	17	16
12		>=	>=	>=	>=	>=	>=	>=	
13	Mean needed	16	10	14	12	16	9	11
14	Actual needed	16	10	14	12	16	9	11
15	Shortage	0	0	0	0	0	0	0
16								
17	shortage?	0						
18				Standard				
19	Mean shortage	0	<=	0.1				

Solution   Our adjustable cells will be the number of employees *starting work on each day of the week*. We proceed as follows:

Step 1: In cells E4:E10 enter trial values for the number of employees starting work each day (E4 is Sunday starters, E5 is Monday starters, ... E10 is Saturday starters).

Step 2: In cells F4:L10 enter a "1" if an employee is working on that day and a "0" if she is not. For example, row 4 refers to workers starting on Sunday, so we have a "1" for Sunday-Thursday and a 0 for Friday and Saturday,

Step 3: In F11:L11 compute the number of people working each day of the week by copying from F11 to G11:L11 the formula

$$=SUMPRODUCT(\$E\$4:\$E\$10,F4:F10).$$

Step 4: In F14:L14 compute the *actual* number of employees needed each day by copying from F14 to G14:L14 the formula

$$=RiskPoisson(F13).$$

Step 5: In F15:L15 we compute the daily shortage of employees by copying from F15 to G15:L15 the formula

$$=MAX(F14-F11,0).$$

Step 6: In F17 we determine if there is any shortage at all with the formula

$$=IF(MAX(F15:L15)>0,1,0).$$

Step 7: In cell F19 we compute the fraction of iterations for each simulation that result in a shortage with the formula

$$=RiskMean(F17).$$

Step 8: In cell E2 we compute the total number of workers with the formula

$$=SUM(E4:E10).$$

Step 9: We can now use RISKOptimizer to determine the minimum number of employees needed to provide adequate service. The Model window is in Figure 11.2.

Figure 11.2

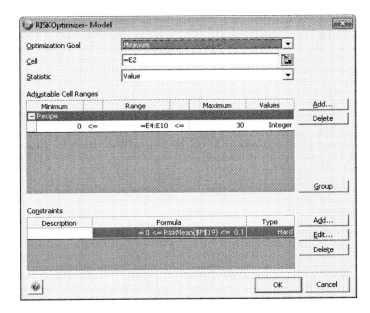

Our goal is to minimize the total number of employees (cell E2). Our Adjustable Cell Ranges are the number of employees starting each day (E4:E10). We constrain the number of employees starting each day to be an integer between 1 and 30. The second constraint ensures that each employee schedule will cause a shortage during at most 10% of all weeks.

From Figure 11.1 we find that RISKOptimizer utilizes 32 workers according to the following schedule:

	D	E
3	Day	Started
4	Sunday	13
5	Monday	3
6	Tuesday	3
7	Wednesday	0
8	Thursday	7
9	Friday	4
10	Saturday	2

This schedule will cause us to have a shortage of employees during around 8% of all weeks.

Using a Cost Structure to Deal with Uncertainty

Another way to approach this problem is to assume that we deal with shortages by paying employees to work overtime. To be more specific, suppose that each employee is paid $700 per week for their regular five day stint, but manpower shortages are made up at a cost of $280 per day short. We now determine a schedule for this situation. See file post2.xls and Figure 11.3.

Figure 11.3

	B	C	D	E	F	G	H	I	J	K	L
1		Ot Wage	RT Wage								
2		280	700	17	Work Matrix						
3				Started	Sunday	Monday	Tuesday	Wednesda	Thursday	Friday	Saturday
4	Cost			0	1	1	1	1	1	0	0
5	RT	11900		6	0	1	1	1	1	1	0
6	OT	7000		3	0	0	1	1	1	1	1
7	total	18900		0	1	0	0	1	1	1	1
8				3	1	1	0	0	1	1	1
9				3	1	1	1	0	0	1	1
10				2	1	1	1	1	0	0	1
11				Mean = 16695	8	14	14	11	12	15	11
12					>=	>=	>=	>=	>=	>=	>=
13				Mean needed	16	10	14	12	16	9	11
14				Actual needed	27	15	13	11	16	8	12
15				Shortage	19	1	0	0	4	0	1
16											
17				Total shortage	25						

Few changes are needed from our previous model.

Step by Step

Step 1: In cell F17 we compute the total shortage for the week with the formula

=SUM(F15:L15).

Step 2: In cell C5 we compute our regular time wage cost for the week with the formula

=D2*E2.

Step 3: In cell C6 we compute our overtime wage cost for the week with the formula

=F17*C2.

Step 4: In cell C7 compute total weekly cost with the formula

=SUM(C5:C6).

Step 5: We are now ready to use RISKOptimizer to find a work schedule that minimizes expected weekly costs. See Figure 11.4.

Figure 11.4

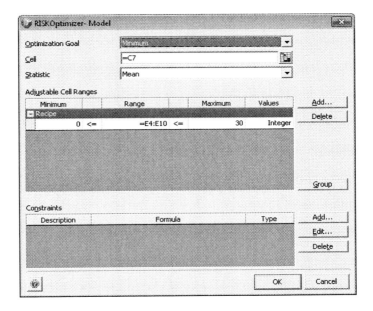

We choose to minimize mean weekly cost (cell C7) by adjusting number of workers starting each day (E4:E10). We assume no more than 30 workers will start each day. RISKOptimizer obtains a mean weekly cost of $16,995 with the following schedule:

	D	E
3	Day	Started
4	Sunday	0
5	Monday	6
6	Tuesday	3
7	Wednesda	0
8	Thursday	3
9	Friday	3
10	Saturday	2

Note a total of 17 employees are needed. This accounts for $11,900 in weekly salary. Therefore, an average of around $5000 in overtime is paid each week. Thus employees work around 18 days of overtime each week, or 1 day of overtime work per employee.

Chapter 12: Job Shop Scheduling

Consider a job shop with a single machine. The length of time needed to complete each job is uncertain. Each job has a known due date. In what order should the jobs be processed? Three reasonable objectives spring to mind:

- Maximize expected number of jobs completed on time.
- Minimize mean total of the tardiness of the jobs.
- Minimize maximum lateness of any job

The following example shows how to solve job shop scheduling problems with RISKOptimizer.

Example 12.1   A small print shop has 10 jobs scheduled. For each job the best case duration, the most likely duration, and the worst case duration is given in Figure 12.1. The due date for each job is also given (see file jobshop1.xls). For example, for Job 1 the best case is that the job will take 5 days, the most likely case is that the job will take 8 days, and the worst case is that Job 1 will take 15 days. Job 1 is due at the end of Day 6.

Figure 12.1

	C	D	E	F	G	H
18	Job	Lowest	Most likely	Worst	Time	Due Date
19	1	5	8	15	7.752926	6
20	2	3	7	12	7.208382	21
21	3	1	3	9	5.15733	46
22	4	2	4	8	4.693512	47
23	5	10	12	18	11.12812	35
24	6	6	8	17	14.58061	66
25	7	2	5	9	5.452041	50
26	8	4	6	11	6.09866	38
27	9	10	11	13	10.30965	14
28	10	6	7	9	7.772322	55

If our goal is to maximize the expected number of jobs completed on time, in what order should the jobs be processed?

To solve this problem we will select the **Order** solution method. For a given set of adjustable cells, the order method will try different permutations of the numbers originally placed in the adjustable cells. For example, if we put the numbers 1, 2, 3, …9, 10 in 10 adjustable cells and select the order method, RISKOptimizer will try different orderings such as 3, 4, 5, 6, 8, 9, 10, 1, 2, 7, etc. These different orderings correspond to different job schedule sequences. We proceed as follows:

Step by Step

Step 1: In cells G19:G28 use the triangular random variable to generate the duration of each job. Copy from G19 to G20:G28 the formula

$$=RiskTriang(D19,E19,F19).$$

Step 2: In cells C5:C14 enter any permutation of the integers 1, 2, …9, 10. This permutation represents a potential job schedule. See Figure 12.2.

Figure 12.2

	B	C	D	E	F	G	H	I
4	Order	Actual job	Actual time	Due Date	Time completed	On time	Time Late	
5	1	2	10.29628014	21	10.29628	1	0	
6	2	5	11.42196385	35	21.718244	1	0	
7	3	8	6.708545465	38	28.426789	1	0	
8	4	4	5.422226365	47	33.849016	1	0	
9	5	3	3.21222167	46	37.061237	1	0	
10	6	10	6.669641845	55	43.730879	1	0	
11	7	7	5.061215362	50	48.792095	1	0	
12	8	1	5.324259711	6	54.116354	0	48.11635	
13	9	6	11.46979883	66	65.586153	1	0	
14	10	9	11.20713324	14	76.793286	0	62.79329	
15					Total	8	110.9096	
16								Mean = 6.86
17								

Thus Figure 2 indicates that Job 2 is done first, then Job 5, … and finally Job 9.

Step 3: Name the cell range C19:H28 Lookup and create the duration of each job in D5:D14 by copying from D5 to D14 the formula

$$=VLOOKUP(\$C5,Lookup,5).$$

Step 4: In E5:E14 compute the due date of each job by copying from E5 to E6:E14 the formula

$$=VLOOKUP(C5,Lookup,6).$$

Step 5: In F5 we compute the time the first job scheduled is completed with the formula

$$=D5.$$

In F6:F14 we compute the time all remaining jobs are completed by copying from F6 to F7:F14 the formula

$$=F5+D6.$$

Step 6: In G5:G14 we determine if each job is completed on time by copying from G5 to G6:G14 the formula

$$=IF(F5<=E5,1,0).$$

Step 7: In H5:H14 we compute the lateness (if any) of each job by copying from H5 to H6:H14 the formula

$$=IF(F5>E5,F5-E5,0).$$

Step 8: In cell G15 we compute the total number of jobs completed on time with the formula

$$=SUM(G5:G14).$$

Copying this formula to H15 computes the total tardiness of the jobs.

Step 9: **We can now use RISKOptimizer to determine a job sequence that maximizes the expected number of jobs completed on time.** Our model is defined as follows:

RISKOptimizer- Model

Optimization Goal   Maximum

Cell   =G15

Statistic   Mean

Adjustable Cell Ranges

Range	
Order	
	=C5:C14

Add...
Delete

Group

Constraints

Description	Formula	Type

Add...
Edit...
Delete

OK   Cancel

RISKOptimizer - Adjustable Cell Group Settings

General | Operators

Definition

Description

Solving Method   Order

Optimization Parameters

Crossover Rate   0.5

Mutation Rate   Automatic

OK   Cancel

Note the selection of Order as Solving Method in the Adjustable Cell Group Settings dialog box. We maximize the mean number of jobs completed on time (G15) by trying different permutations of C5:C14. From Figure 12.1 we find that the best schedule averages completing 6.65 jobs on time. The optimal sequence found is 2, 5, 8, 4, 3, 10, 7, 1, 6, and 9.

Minimizing Total Lateness

To minimize total mean lateness, just minimize the mean of H15. The schedule minimizing total mean lateness is shown in Figure 12.3. See file jobshop2.xls.

Figure 12.3

	B	C	D	E	F	G	H	I	J	K
4	Order	Actual job	Actual time	Due Date	Time completed	On time	Time Late			
5	1	1	13.39670324	6	13.396703	0	7.396703			
6	2	9	10.2931101	14	23.689813	0	9.689813			
7	3	2	6.738356656	21	30.42817	0	9.42817			
8	4	8	6.91709829	38	37.345268	1	0			
9	5	3	5.289887288	46	42.635156	1	0			
10	6	4	5.109756749	47	47.744912	0	0.744912			
11	7	7	6.164431741	50	53.909344	0	3.909344			
12	8	10	7.01683453	55	60.926179	0	5.926179			
13	9	6	14.53080922	66	75.456988	0	9.456988			
14	10	5	12.0650782	35	87.522066	0	52.52207			
15					Total	2	99.07418			
16										
17										
18		Job	Lowest	Most likely	Worst	Time	Due Date		Mean = 68.6946	
19		1	5	8	15	13.3967	6			

The smallest mean total tardiness is 68.69 days. This is obtained by sequencing the jobs in the following order: 1, 9, 2, 8, 3, 4, 7, 10, 6, 5.

Minimizing Maximum Lateness

If we want to find a schedule minimizing the average of the maximum time a job is late simply change the formula in H15 to

$= MAX(H5:H14).$

Then choose to minimize the mean of cell H15. The result is given in Figure 12.4.

Figure 12.4

	B	C	D	E	F	G	H	I
4	Order	Actual job	Actual time	Due Date	Time completed	On time	Time Late	
5	1	1	10.85552013	6	10.85552	0	4.85552	
6	2	9	10.20998058	14	21.065501	0	7.065501	
7	3	2	7.049275498	21	28.114776	0	7.114776	
8	4	5	14.65422483	35	42.769001	0	7.769001	
9	5	8	5.385406989	38	48.154408	0	10.15441	
10	6	3	7.010544722	46	55.164953	0	9.164953	
11	7	7	5.741853783	50	60.906807	0	10.90681	
12	8	10	7.122078069	55	68.028885	0	13.02888	
13	9	4	4.716404256	47	72.745289	0	25.74529	
14	10	6	10.27340105	66	83.01869	0	17.01869	
15						max	25.74529	
16								Mean =
17								22.8396
18		Job	Lowest	Most likely	Worst	Time	Due Date	

By scheduling the jobs in the sequence 1, 9, 2, 5, 8, 3, 7, 10, 4, and 6 we obtain a mean maximum lateness of 22.84 days.

Chapter 13: Optimal Sampling

Determining an optimal sample plan is a tricky matter. A company incurs a cost when a "bad" batch of a product passes inspection or a "good" batch fails inspection. Unfortunately the only way to prevent (with 100% certainty) a good batch from failing and a bad batch from passing is to completely inspect the batch. The following example shows how RISKOptimizer can be used to determine a cost minimizing sampling plan.

Example 13.1   Fruit Computer ships computers in batches of 10,000. The number of defective computers in a batch follows a Poisson random variable with mean 20. A batch is considered acceptable if it contains 15 or fewer defective computers. It costs Fruit $0.50 to inspect a computer. Fruit estimates that a cost of $3000 is incurred if a bad batch is sent out after inspection. A cost of $1000 is incurred if a good batch fails inspection. This is due to the fact that a batch failing inspection will be completely reworked. What sampling plan minimizes expected cost per batch?

Solution   A sampling plan is defined by two parameters:

- A sample size N
- A cutoff point c. If c or fewer defectives are found in our sample of size N, the batch is accepted. Otherwise the batch is rejected.

We insert trial values of N and c in our spreadsheet and determine for a random batch the cost of sampling, the cost due to a bad batch passing, and the cost of a good batch failing. Then we use RISKOptimizer to minimize the mean cost per batch. Our work is in Figure 13.1. See the file Sampling.xls.

Figure 13.1

	A	B	C	D	E
1	Sampling	Ok<=15	Bad>15		
2					
3	Number of defectives	22			
4					
5	Sample size	951			
6	cut off point	0			
7	cost per unit tested	$ 0.50			
8	cost if good batch rejected	$ 1,000.00			
9	cost if bad batch gets through	$ 3,000.00			
10	**Result of batch**				
11	Sample result	2			
12	Sample Passes?	0	0=fails; 1= passes		
13	Good batch was rejected	0			
14	Bad batch was accepted	0			
15	**Cost per batch**				
16	Sampling cost	$ 475.50			
17	Cost of bad batch passing	$ -			
18	Cost of good batch failing	$ -			
19	Total cost	$ 475.50			
20					
21					
22					
23				Mean = 937.1667	
24					

Step 1: In cell B3 we compute the number of defectives in a batch with the formula

$=RiskPoisson(20).$

Step 2: In cell B5 and B6 we enter trial values for the sample size and cutoff point.

Step 3: In B7:B9 we enter the cost parameters for the problem.

Step 4: In cell B11 we use the *hypergeometric random variable* to generate the number of defectives in the sample. The formula

$=RiskHypergeo(n,d,N)$

will generate the number of defectives in a sample of size n from a batch of N items which contains d defective items.

With this syntax the number of defectives in our sample is computed with the formula

$=RiskHypergeo(B5,B3,10000).$

Step 5: In cell B12 we ensure that the batch passes if and only if the number of defectives in the sample does not exceed the cutoff. Note a "1" indicates a batch passes while a "0" indicates a batch fails.

=IF(B11<=B6,1,0).

Step 6: In cell B13 we place a "1" if and only if a good batch (<=15 total defectives in batch) fails inspection with the formula

=IF(AND(B12=0,B3<=15),1,0).

Step 7: In cell B14 we place a "1" if and only if a bad batch (>16 defectives in whole batch) passes inspection with the formula

=IF(AND(B12=1,B3>15),1,0).

Step 8: In cell B16 we compute the cost of sampling with the formula

=B7*B5.

Step 9: In cell B17 we compute the cost incurred if a bad batch passes with the formula

=B14*B9.

Step 10: In cell B18 we compute the cost incurred if a good batch fails with the formula

=B8*B13.

Step 11: In cell B19 we incur the total cost for the batch with the formula

=SUM(B16:B18).

Step 12: **We can now use RISKOptimizer to minimize expected cost per batch.** Our Model window looks as follows:

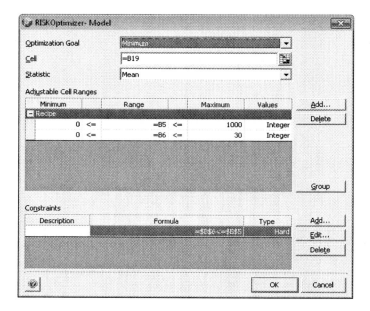

We minimize the mean cost per batch (B19) by adjusting sample size (B5) and cutoff point (B6). Both adjustable cells must be integers between 0 and 10,000 with the cutoff point being less than or equal to the sample size. From Figure 13.1 we find mean expected cost per batch is minimized at a value of $937 by sampling 951 computers and passing a batch if and only if no defective computers are found. Note complete inspection would cost $5000 per batch!

Chapter 14: Periodic Review Inventory Model

In many situations a business reviews inventory periodically and determines whether to place an order, and (if an order is placed), the size of the order. Let's assume that inventory is reviewed each week and the business incurs the following types of costs:

- **Fixed ordering cost** - Each time an order is placed a fixed cost K is incurred. This cost is independent of the order size.
- **Unit purchase cost** - A cost P per unit ordered is incurred.
- **Unit holding cost** - A cost H is incurred for each unit in inventory at the end of a given period.
- **Unit shortage cost** - A cost SC is incurred each time period for each unit of demand that is unmet at the end of a time period.

Assume the firm is able to backlog demand, that is unmet demand may be met during a later period. It can be shown that for a periodic review inventory model the expected average cost per period over a long time horizon is minimized by an (s, S) policy. In an (s, S) policy an order is placed at the beginning of any period in which beginning inventory is less than s. The size of the order is the amount needed to bring inventory (if delivery of order is immediate) up to S. The following example shows how to use RISKOptimizer to determine an optimal (s, S) policy.

Example 14.1 A company has a periodic review (weekly) inventory system with the following parameter values:

- K = $200
- P = $4
- H = $3
- SC = $10.

Weekly demand for the product follows a Poisson random variable with a mean of 30 units per week. An order is equally likely to arrive 1, 2, or 3 weeks after it is placed. At the beginning of Week 1 100 units are in stock. Determine an (s, S) policy that minimizes expected costs over 40 weeks.

Solution

Our work is in the file Inventory.xls. See Figure 14.1. Each week we keep track of the following quantities:

- **Beginning inventory**: This is the inventory after an order (if any) is received, but before demand is met.
- **Quantity on order**: This equals 0 if nothing is on order. Otherwise it equals the size of the order that is in process.
- **Next order received**: If no order is in process, we set this equal to a large number (9999). Otherwise, Next order received is the week in which our in process order arrives. Of course, the week the next order is received is random.
- **Demand**: Weekly demand for the product is modeled with the function =RiskPoisson(30).
- **Ending Inventory**: This is our inventory after all possible demand has been met. A negative ending inventory means a shortage has occurred.
- **Purchasing cost**: During a period in which an order is placed, the ordering cost equals $200 plus $4 for each item ordered.
- **Holding cost**: If ending inventory is positive, then holding cost equals 3*(ending inventory). Otherwise holding cost equals 0.
- **Shortage cost**: If ending inventory is negative, shortage cost equals 10*(-ending inventory). Otherwise shortage cost equals 0.

Figure 14.1

	A	B	C	D	E	F	G	H	AL	AM	AN	AO
1	Shortage cost	$ 10.00		Inventory								
2	Holding cost	$ 3.00		Model								
3	Fixed cost	$ 200.00		with								
4	Unit Purchasing cost	$ 4.00		Random								
5	Order up to	137		Leadtime								
6	Reorder point	76										
7												
8	Week	1	2	3	4	5	6	7	37	38	39	40
9	Beginning inventory	100	78	52	104	84	53	23	30	-2	53	17
10	Quantity on order	0	0	85	0	0	84	84	78	78	84	84
11	Next Order received	9999	9999	4	9999	9999	8	8	39	39	42	42
12	Demand	22	26	33	20	31	30	22	32	23	36	42
13	Ending Inventory	78	52	19	84	53	23	1	-2	-25	17	-25
14	Order cost	$ -	0	540	0	0	536	0	0	0	0	0
15	Holding cost	234	156	57	252	159	69	3	0	0	51	0
16	Shortage cost	0	0	0	0	0	0	0	20	250	0	250
17	Total Cost	$ 234.00	$ 156.00	$ 597.00	$	252.00	$ 159.00	$ 605.00	$ 3.00	$ 20.00	$ 250.00	$ 51.00	$ 250.00
18												
19	Total Cost	$13,575.00										
20												
21												
22				Mean = 13261.563								
23												

We now proceed as follows:

Step by Step

Step 1: In A1:B4 we enter cost parameters.

Step 2: In A5:B6 we enter trial values of s and S.

Step 3: In B10 we compute the quantity on order for week 1 with the formula

   =IF(B9<$B$6,$B$5-B9,0).

This ensures that an order (which brings our inventory up to S, assuming instantaneous arrival) is placed if and only if the beginning inventory is less than the reorder point. Since Week 1 beginning inventory is not less than our trial value of s, no order is placed.

Step 4: We now keep track of the next week in which an order is received. If no order is in process, we make the next time an order is received a very large number (9999). If an order is placed, we generate the duration of the time needed to process the order (the *lead time*) with the =RISKDISCRETE function and record the arrival date of the order. Entering the following statement in B11 accomplishes these goals.

   =IF(B10=0,9999,B8+RiskDiscrete({1,2,3},{1,1,1})).

Step 5: We now generate week 1 demand in B12 with the formula

   =RiskPoisson(30).

Step 6: The firm's ending inventory for Week 1 equals beginning inventory less demand. We compute Week 1 ending inventory in B13 with the formula

   =B9-B12.

Step 7: In cell B14 we compute the cost associated with the Week 1 order (if any) with the formula

   *=IF(B10>0,$B$3,0)+$B$4*B10.*

This formula picks up the fixed cost of K if and only if an order is placed and pays $P per unit purchased.

Step 8: In cell B15 we compute our Week 1 holding cost by multiplying H times ending inventory with the formula

   *=IF(B13>0,B13*$B$2,0).*

Step 9: In cell B16 we compute our Week 1 shortage cost by multiplying S times our ending shortage with the formula

   =IF(B13<0,-B13*$B$1,0).

Step 10: In cell B17 compute Week 1 total cost with the formula

   =SUM(B14:B16).

Step 11: In C9 we compute Week 2's beginning inventory by adding the size of an arriving order (if any) to Week 1 ending inventory with the formula

   =B13+IF(B11=C8,B10,0).

Step 12: If the quantity ordered during Week 1 is scheduled to arrive later than Week 2, then Quantity on order for Week 2 = Quantity on order for Week 1. If this is not the case and we begin Week 2 with inventory below the reorder point, an order must be placed. Otherwise, an order has arrived this week or nothing is on order, and Week 2 quantity on order = 0. **The following statement in C10 operationalizes this logic:**

   =IF(AND((B11<42),(B11>C8)),B10,IF(C9<$B$6,$B$5-C9,0)).

Step 13: If nothing is on order, we make the week the next order arrives equal to 9999. If an order has just been placed this week (this is the case only if (C10 - B10) > 0), then we must update the arrival of the next order by generating a random lead-time with the *RiskDuniform* function. Otherwise, we are still waiting for an order, and the value of Next Order Received remains unchanged. **These relationships are captured in cell C11 with the formula**

   =IF(C10=0,9999,IF(ABS(C10-B10)>0,C8+RiskDuniform({1,2,3}),B11)).

Step 14: In cells C12:C17 we simply copy the formulas in B12:B17.

Step 15: Copying from the cell range C9:C17 to D9:AN17 simulates 40 weeks.

Step 16: In cell B19 we compute total cost with the formula

   =SUM(B17:AO17).

Step 17: **We are now ready to use RISKOptimizer to find the (s, S) policy that minimizes expected cost over 40 weeks.** Our Model window is below.

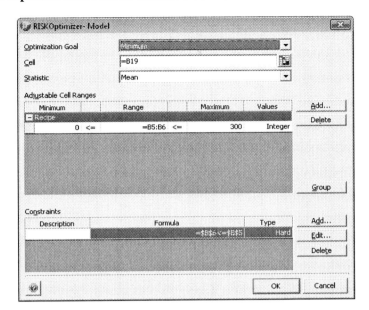

We choose to minimize the mean of total cost (cell B19). Our adjustable cells are S (B5) and s (B6). We constrain s and S to be between 0 and 300 (assume we cannot store more than 300 units). Also, we must have s<=S so we add the simulation constraint B6<=B5. As shown in Figure 1, RISKOptimizer recommends s = 76 and S = 137. Thus any week in which beginning inventory is 75 or less an order is placed to bring inventory (assuming 0 lead-time) to 137. This policy will incur a mean cost for 40 weeks of $13,262.

Chapter 15: Truck Loading

Certain optimization models involve assigning items into one of several groups. Here are some examples:

- A football game has 12 two-minute breaks for commercials. Clients have ads of varying lengths that they want to assign to these "breaks". How can we maximize the revenue earned from the ads assigned to these breaks?
- A will leaves 20 companies to eight heirs. How can we assign the companies, so that (as closely as possible) each heir gets companies of equal value?

RISKOptimizer has built in a solution method (**grouping**) which is useful for these situations. Here is an example.

Example 15.1   Federal Shipping picks up packages at 20 locations. At the beginning of the day Federal does not know the weight of the packages that will have to be picked up at each location, but based on historical data they have an idea about the mean weight of the packages at each location. See Figure 15.1 and file truck.xls. The standard deviation of the weight of the packages at each location is about 20% of the mean. Federal has six trucks that can each handle 180 pounds. How should Federal assign locations to trucks to minimize the expected amount by which trucks are overloaded?

Figure 15.1

	A	B	C	D	E	F	G	H	I	J
1	Site	Mean	Actual	Truck		Capacity	180			
2	1	91	82.01508	1		Truck	Total	Over?	Means	
3	2	32	21.49645	4		1	162.4356	0	163	
4	3	9	10.06623	1		2	198.326	18.32595	210	
5	4	60	56.99225	2		3	172.3126	0	166	
6	5	50	40.98209	4		4	147.527	0	160	
7	6	84	113.2159	5		5	197.6234	17.62343	168	
8	7	43	35.77453	6		6	178.0434	0	166	
9	8	67	73.99972	6						
10	9	80	79.4595	2			Total	35.94938		
11	10	7	7.852164	3						
12	11	71	78.78759	3						
13	12	46	46.29887	4					Mean = 44.3528	
14	13	84	84.4075	5						
15	14	18	18.25908	3						
16	15	63	70.3543	1						
17	16	70	61.8742	2						
18	17	47	43.00782	3						
19	18	23	24.40598	3						
20	19	32	38.74957	4						
21	20	56	68.26913	6						
22			1056.268							

The key to our model will be the use of the =SUMIF function to determine how much weight is picked up by each truck. We proceed as follows:

Step 1: In cells C2:C21 we compute the actual weight at each location. Assuming the weight at each site is normally distributed, we simply copy from C2 to C3:C21 the formula

$$=RiskNormal(B2,0.2*B2).$$

Step 2: In cells D2:D21 enter trial values (integers between 1 and 6). These numbers represent the truck assigned to the given site.

Step 3: In G3:G8 compute the total weight actually picked up by each truck by copying from G3 to G4:G8 the formula

$$=SUMIF(\$D\$2:\$D\$21,F3,\$C\$2:\$C\$21).$$

This formula sums all numbers in C2:C21 for which the number in column D equals F3. This is, of course, the actual weight of all sites assigned to truck 1.

Step 4: In H3:H8 compute the amount by which each truck is overloaded by copying from H3 to H4:H8 the formula

$$=IF(G3>\$G\$1,G3-\$G\$1,0).$$

Step 5: In H10 we compute the total amount by which the trucks are overloaded with the formula

$$=SUM(H3:H8).$$

Step 6: We are now ready to use RISKOptimizer to determine the assignment of trucks to sites that minimizes expected truck overloading. Our Model window is shown in Figure 15.2.

Figure 15.2

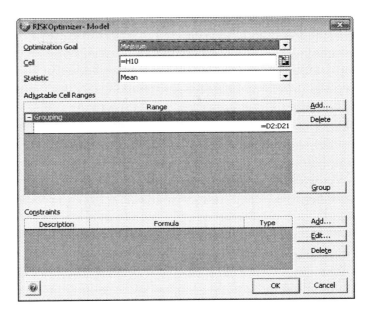

We choose to minimize the mean overloading of trucks (cell H10) by adjusting the cells D2:D21. Note from the Adjustable Cell Group Settings dialog box below we selected GROUPING as the Solving Method.

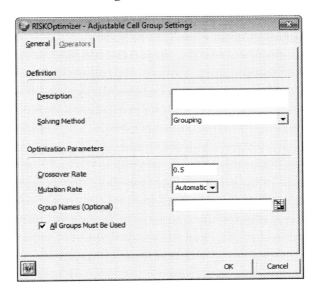

The GROUPING method ensures that on each simulation RISKOptimizer will choose the values in D2:D21 *from the values initially inserted in those cells*. In other words, since we initially put the integers 1, 2, ... 6 in D2:D21 this will remain true for each simulation. RISKOptimizer found an average overloading of trucks of 44.35 pounds by assigning the trucks as shown in Figure 15.1:

- Truck 1 to sites 1, 3, and 15.
- Truck 2 to sites 4, 9, and 16.
- Truck 3 to sites 10, 11, 14, 17 and 18.
- Truck 4 to sites 2, 5, 12, and 19.
- Truck 5 to sites 6 and 13.
- Truck 6 to sites 7, 8, and 20.

Note from Column I of Figure 15.1 how RISKOptimizer allocated virtually the same mean demand to Truck 1 and Trucks 3-6. RISKOptimizer opted to slightly overload Truck 1.

Chapter 16: Determining Optimal Capacity for a New Product

One of the most important decisions a company must make is the capacity assigned to a new product. When a new product comes out, demand is highly uncertain. Too little capacity results in reduced profit due to lost sales while too much capacity results in higher fixed costs than necessary. In this chapter we show how RISKOptimizer can be used to address the capacity planning decision. We note that forecasting new sales of a product is discussed in Chapter 36 of Winston (1998).

Example 16.1   Drugco needs to determine the proper capacity level for a new drug, Niagara. Our goal is to maximize the expected NPV earned from the drug during years 0-14. Assume a discount rate of 10% per year. It costs $10 to build enough capacity to produce one unit of drug per year. All construction cost is incurred during Year 0. It costs $.10 per year to maintain a unit of annual production capacity. In Year 1 we know demand will be for 160,000 units of Niagara. We believe that the mean annual percentage growth of demand for Niagara is unknown and equally likely to assume any value between 10% and 20%. Actual growth rate of demand during any year is normally distributed with the given mean and a standard deviation of 6%.

During Year 1 each unit of Niagara sells for $8.00. The price of Niagara will almost surely grow at 5% per year. Unit variable cost is known to be 40% of sales price. What capacity level will maximize expected discounted profit? We assume all building costs are during Year 0 and all cash flows occur at the beginning of the year.

Solution   Our work is in the file capacity1.xls. We assume that the drug perishes at the end of each year, so excess capacity cannot be used to build inventory for future years.
Each year sales will equal minimum of *(demand, capacity)*. See Figure 16.1. Only Years 1-4 are shown.

Figure 16.1

	A	B	C	D	E	F	G	O	P
1	Capacity	411000							
2	mean growth	0.15							
3	sigma growth	0.06							
4	unit building cost	$ 10.00							
5	annual unit maintenance cost	$ 1.00							
6	year 1 sales	160000							
7	year 1 price	$ 8.00							
8	cost/price	0.4							
9	inflation	0.05							
10	interest rate	0.1							
11									
12	Year	0	1	2	3	4	5	13	14
13	Capacity		411000	411000	411000	411000	411000	411000	411000
14	Building cost	$ 4,110,000.00							
15	Annual Maintenance cost		$ 411,000.00	$ 411,000.00	$ 411,000.00	$ 411,000.00	$ 411,000.00	$ 411,000.00	$ 411,000.00
16	Demand		160000	184000	211600	243340	279841	856040.0169	984446.0194
17	Units sold		160000	184000	211600	243340	279841	411000	411000
18	Unit price		$8.00	$8.40	$8.82	$9.26	$9.72	$14.37	$15.09
19	Unit variable cost		$ 3.20	$ 3.36	$ 3.53	$ 3.70	$ 3.89	$ 5.75	$ 6.03
20	Annual Variable cost		$ 512,000.00	$ 618,240.00	$ 746,524.80	$ 901,428.70	$ 1,088,475.15	$ 2,361,910.24	$ 2,480,005.75
21	Annual Sales revenue		$ 1,280,000.00	$ 1,545,600.00	$ 1,866,312.00	$ 2,253,571.74	$ 2,721,187.88	$ 5,904,775.60	$ 6,200,014.38
22	Profit	$ (4,110,000.00)	$ 357,000.00	$ 516,360.00	$ 708,787.20	$ 941,143.04	$ 1,221,712.73	$ 3,131,865.36	$ 3,309,008.63
23									
24									
25	NPV	$ 7,358,307.02							
26									
27									
28					Mean = 7155692.9563				
29									
30	Trial								
31									
32									
33									
34									
35									
36									
37									
38									

Step by Step

Step 1: In cell B1 enter a trial value for capacity.

Step 2: In cell B2 model the mean annual growth rate of demand with the formula

=RiskUniform(.10, .20).

Step 3: In B3:B10 enter relevant parameters for the problem.

Step 4: In cell B14 compute the cost of building the plant with the formula

=B1*B4.

Step 5: In C13:P13 compute capacity available each year by copying

=$B$12

from C13 to D13:P13.

Step 6: In C15:P15 compute the annual cost of maintaining capacity by copying from C15 to D15:P15 the formula

=C13*$B$5.

Step 7: In C16 compute Year 1 demand with the formula

$= B6.$

Step 8: In D16:P16 compute demand for Years 2-14 by copying the formula

$=C16*RiskNormal(1+\$B\$2,\$B\$3)$

from D16 to E16:P16.

Step 9: In C17:P17 we compute the units sold each year by copying from C17 to D17:P17 the formula

$=MIN(C16,C13).$

Step 10: In C18:P18 we compute unit price of product. In C18 we compute Year 1 unit price with formula

$=B7.$

We compute the unit price for years 2-14 by copying the formula

$=C18*(1+\$B\$9)$

from D18:P18.

Step 11: In C19:P19 we compute the unit variable cost by copying from C19 to D19:P19 the formula

$=\$B\$8*C18.$

Step 12: In C20:P20 we compute annual variable cost by copying from C20 to D20:P20 the formula

$=C19*C17.$

Step 13: In C21:P21 compute annual sales revenue by copying from C21 to D21:P21 the formula

$=C18*C17.$

Step 14: In B22:P22 we compute the profit for each year by copying from B22 to C22:P22 the formula

$=B21-B20-B15-B14.$

Step 15: In B25 we compute the NPV of all our cash flows with the formula

$$=B22 + NPV(B10,C22:P22).$$

Step 16: We are now ready to use RISKOptimizer to find the capacity level that maximizes expected NPV. Our RISKOptimizer Model window follows:

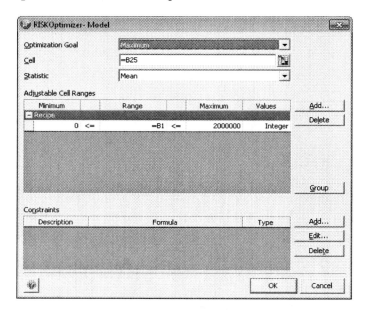

We choose to maximize mean NPV (cell B25) by adjusting capacity level (cell B1). We constrain capacity to be an integer between 0 and 2,000,000. From Figure 16.1 we find that expected NPV is maximized (at $7.16 million) by a capacity of 411,000 units.

Allowing Flexibility in the Capacity Decision

Now let's suppose that Drugco has the opportunity to review demand during Year 5 and, if desired build additional capacity. How will this change Drugco's strategy? Now Drugco does not need to build as much capacity during Year 1 because they can wait and see if demand will be high. If demand is high, they can ramp up capacity during Year 5 for future years; if not they can stick with their Year 1 capacity. To model this situation we assume that after observing Year 5 demand Drugco proceeds as follows: If ratio of Year 5 demand to capacity exceeds some cutoff point C, then Drugco will add capacity. If capacity is added then Drugco will add enough capacity to bring total capacity to a multiple M of Year 5 demand. We assume it costs $12 to build one unit of capacity at the end of Year 5. Thus Drugco's capacity strategy is defined by three adjustable cells:

- Initial Year 1 Capacity.
- Cutoff point C which defines if capacity is added after Year 5 (assume capacity arrives in time for Year 6).
- A multiple M that defines how much capacity is added.

Note that the effects of the three adjustable cells are linked; if we add a lot of capacity now we will not need to add much later. If we are willing to add a lot of capacity later we do not need much now. We can use RISKOptimizer to find the optimal strategy of this type. Our work is in Figure 16.2 and file cap2.xls.

Solution   We modify our previous worksheet as follows:

Step by Step   **Step 1: In D1 and D2 enter trial values for C and M. In D3 enter unit cost of adding capacity during Year 5.**

Step 2: Insert three rows below Row 13. These rows will be used to model the addition of capacity during Year 5.

Step 3: In G14 and G15 we determine if any capacity will be added. In G14 we determine the ratio of current demand to capacity with the formula

   =G19/G13.

If the ratio in G14 exceeds the cutoff in D1, we add capacity. To model this we enter in cell G15 the formula

   =IF(G14>D1,"Yes","No").

Figure 16.2

	A	B	C	D	E	F	G	H
1	Capacity	194730	Cutoff ratio	1.002611				
2	mean growth	0.15	Percentage added	2.582837				
3	sigma growth	0.06	Cost of adding	12				
4	unit building	$ 10.00						
5	annual unit maintenance	$ 1.00						
6	year 1 sales	160000						
7	year 1 price	$ 8.00						
8	cost/price	0.4						
9	inflation	0.05						
10	interest rate	0.1						
11								
12	Year	0	1	2	3	4	5	6
13	Capacity		194730	194730	194730	194730	194730	722783.73
14	Sales/Capacity						1.4370718	
15	Make cut?						Yes	
16	Amount added						528053.73	
17	Building cost	1.95E+06					6336644.8	
18	Annual Maintenance		1.95E+05	1.95E+05	1.95E+05	1.95E+05	1.95E+05	1.95E+05
19	Demand		1.60E+05	1.84E+05	2.12E+05	2.43E+05	2.80E+05	3.22E+05
20	Units sold		1.60E+05	1.84E+05	1.95E+05	1.95E+05	1.95E+05	3.22E+05
21	Unit price	$	8.00	$8.40	$8.82	$9.26	$9.72	$10.21
22	Unit variable	$	3.20	$ 3.36	$ 3.53	$ 3.70	$ 3.89	$ 4.08
23	Annual		5.12E+05	6.18E+05	6.87E+05	7.21E+05	7.57E+05	1.31E+06
24	Annual Sales revenue		1.28E+06	1.55E+06	1.72E+06	1.80E+06	1.89E+06	3.29E+06
25	Profit	-1.95E+06	5.73E+05	7.33E+05	8.36E+05	8.87E+05	-5.40E+06	1.78E+06
26								
27								
28	NPV	$ 10,322,392.00						
29								
30								
31								
32				Mean = 9973786.9271				

Step 4: **In cell G16 we ensure that if any capacity is added, we add enough to bring capacity to a multiple M of current demand.**

=IF(G15="Yes",G19*D2 -G13,0).

Step 5: **In G17 we compute the cost (if any) of adding capacity with the formula**

=G16*D3.

Step 6: **In cell H13 we compute our Year 6 capacity with the formula**

=G13+G16.

Copying this formula to the range I13:P13 computes capacity available for Years 7-14.

Step 7: We are now ready to use RISKOptimizer to determine a strategy that maximizes expected NPV. Our Model window follows:

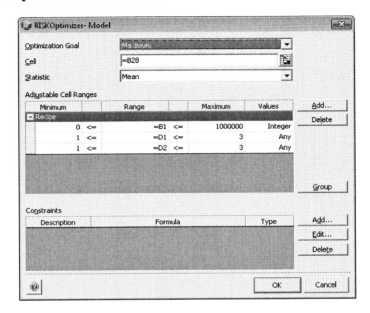

We choose to maximize mean NPV (cell B28) by adjusting Year 1 capacity (B1) our cutoff ratio for adding capacity in Year 5 (D1) and the multiple of current demand that determines our post Year 5 capacity (D2). We constrain our Year 1 capacity to be at most 1,000,000. We constrain both C and M to be between 1 and 3. As shown in Figure 15.2 RISKOptimizer obtains an expected NPV of $9.97 million. The strategy used is to build 194,730 units of capacity now and after observing Year 5 demand add capacity if Year 5 Demand/current capacity is at least 1.002. Then add enough capacity to bring capacity up to 2.58 times Year 5 demand.

Remarks

Note that the addition of flexibility has increased our mean NPV by almost $3 million. Sensibly, with flexibility we build less capacity initially because we have the opportunity to ramp up later.

Reference

Winston, W.L., *Financial Models Using Simulation and Optimization*, Palisade, 1998.

Chapter 17: Capital Budgeting with Uncertain Resource Usage

Each year companies must determine what projects to undertake. Most companies want to maximize the NPV contributed by the selected projects, subject to resource limitations. The problem is, however, that the resource usage of each project is uncertain. RISKOptimizer makes it easy to model this type of problem.

Example 17.1   Chandler Corporation must determine which projects to undertake during the current year. Ten projects are under consideration. A simulation has given Chandler estimates of the NPV of each project. Each project uses an uncertain amount of manpower (in thousands of hours) and capital (in millions of dollars). See Figure 17.1 and file capbud.xls.

We are given the lowest, most likely and highest resource usage for each project. For example, if things go well Project 1 will require $14 million, the most likely case is that Project 1 will require $35 million, and the worst case is that Project 1 will require $55 million.

Chandler wants to maximize mean NPV subject to the constraint that they want to have at most a 5% chance of using more capital or labor than is available. 70,000 man-hours and $85 million are available. Which projects should Chandler select?

Solution   Our adjustable cells will be 0-1 integers for each project. A "1" indicates that a project is selected and a "0" indicates that a project is not selected.

Figure 17.1

	B	C	D	E	F	G	H	I	J
2	Project Selection								
3					NPV				
4			NPV	Chosen?	105				
5		1	55	0	Manpower used		Manpower available	Shortage	Prob Short
6		2	32	0	46.666667		Mean = 105 70	0	0.0000
7		3	47	1					
8		4	7	1	Capital used		Capital available		
9		5	5	0	68.333333		85	0	0.0420
10		6	40	0					
11		7	30	1					
12		8	54	0					
13		9	21	1					
14		10	88	0					
15									
16									
17	Manpower	Lowest	Most likely	Highest	Actual				
18	1	10	22	40	24				
19	2	3	5	16	8				
20	3	12	21	30	21				
21	4	3	5	7	5				
22	5	2	4	6	4				
23	6	9	18	20	15.666667				
24	7	8	10	12	10				
25	8	12	24	40	25.333333				
26	9	6	6	20	10.666667				
27	10	19	32	50	33.666667				
28									
29	Capital	Lowest	Most likely	Highest	Actual				
30	1	14	35	55	34.666667				
31	2	10	21	32	21				
32	3	12	30	47	29.666667				
33	4	4	5	8	5.6666667				
34	5	4	4	10	6				
35	6	14	26	50	30				
36	7	11	16	34	20.333333				
37	8	19	30	56	35				
38	9	5	10	23	12.666667				
39	10	28	56	98	60.666667				

Step by Step

Step 1: Put trial 0-1 values in cells E5:E14.

Step 2: Assuming a triangular distribution governs resource usage, determine the actual manpower usage of each project by copying the formula

$=RiskTriang(C18,D18,E18)$

from F18 to F19:F27.

To generate actual capital usage of each project copy the formula

=*RiskTriang(C30,D30,E30)*

from F30 to F31:F39.

Step 3: In F4 compute total NPV earned by selected projects with the formula

=*SUMPRODUCT(D5:D14,E5:E14).*

Step 4: In F6 compute total manpower used by selected projects with the formula

=*SUMPRODUCT(E5:E14,F18:F27).*

Step 5: In F9 compute total capital usage by selected projects with the formula

=*SUMPRODUCT(E5:E14,F30:F39).*

Step 6: In I6 we determine if a manpower shortage occurs with the formula

=*IF(F6>H6,1,0).*

Similarly in I9 we determine if a capital shortage occurs with the formula

=*IF(F9>H9,1,0).*

Step 7: In J6 we tell RISKOptimizer to keep track of the probability of a manpower shortage on a given simulation with the formula

=*RiskMean(I6).*

Similarly, in J9 we compute the probability of a capital shortage with the formula

=*RiskMean(I9).*

Step 8: **We are now ready to use RISKOptimizer to determine the projects which maximize mean NPV and yield at most a 5% chance of overusing a resource.** Our Model window is below.

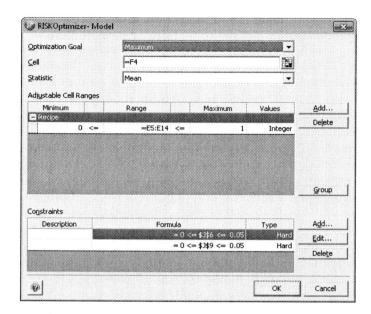

We choose to maximize mean NPV (we could actually use value here) in cell F4 by adjusting F5:F14. We constrain F5:F14 to be 0 or 1. By adding simulation constraints that J6 and J9 are less than or equal to .05 we ensure that our selected projects will only have at most a 5% chance of using too much capital or manpower.

As shown in Figure 17.1, we select Projects 3, 4, 7, and 9. This earns an NPV of $105 million. There is no chance of a manpower shortage, but a 4.2% chance of a capital shortage.

Chapter 18: The Miller-Orr Cash Management Model

Consider a business that experiences uncertain cash flows each week. A crucial decision is how much cash to keep available. If we keep too little cash available, we can run out of cash. If we keep too much cash on hand, we are losing the opportunity to earn interest or income on invested cash. If we adjust our cash level daily, however, we are overwhelmed by transaction costs. Miller and Orr (1966) devised a cash management model for such situations. Under the Miller-Orr model, the business specifies a minimum cash level below which they do not want their cash level to go. Then Miller-Orr specify a cash management policy by two parameters U and T. If our cash on hand exceeds U, then we transfer enough cash into investments to bring our beginning cash to a target T. If our cash on hand drops below the minimum level (call it M), then we transfer enough money out of securities and into cash to bring our cash level to the target T. Here is an example of how to use RISKOptimizer to determine an optimal cash management policy.

Example 18.1   Bank 24's daily cash inflows are normally distributed with a mean of 0 and a standard deviation of $10,000. Bank 24 wants to never have less than $15,000 on hand. Adjusting their cash level incurs a transaction cost of $30. They initially have $100,000 invested in money market funds. Money market funds earn daily interest of .025%. Determine a target T and an upper limit U that maximize B24's expected profit. At the beginning of Day 1 Bank 24 has $28,000 cash on hand.

Solution   We will model the situation for 100 days. See Figure 18.1 and file Miller.xls.

Figure 18.1

	A	B	C	D	E	F	G	H
1	**Miller-Orr Model**							
2	Transaction cost	30						
3	Daily mean	0						
4	Daily sigma	10000						
5	Min cash balance	15000		0.09125				
6	Upper Limit	65992						
7	Target	28063			Profit	2525		
8	Interest rate/day	0.00025						
9	Day	Beginning cash balance	Invest More?	Sell securities?	Transaction Cost	Cash flow	Change in cash from transactions	Ending Cash balance (no int.) — Mean = 2021.5645
10	0	28000	no	no	0	0	0	28000
11	1	28025	no	no	0	0	0	28025
12	2	28050	no	no	0	0	0	28050
13	3	28075	no	no	0	0	0	28075
14	4	28100	no	no	0	0	0	28100
15	5	28125	no	no	0	0	0	28125
16	6	28150	no	no	0	0	0	28150
17	7	28175	no	no	0	0	0	28175
18	8	28200	no	no	0	0	0	28200
19	9	28225	no	no	0	0	0	28225
20	10	28250	no	no	0	0	0	28250
21	11	28275	no	no	0	0	0	28275
22	12	28300	no	no	0	0	0	28300

Step by Step

	H	I	J	K
9	Ending Cash balance(no int.)	Beginning Security balance	Ending Security Balance	Interest earned
10	24607.037	100000	100000	25
11	21089.176	100000	100000	25
12	18907.479	100000	100000	25
13	20099.849	100000	100000	25
14	18503.787	100000	100000	25
15	18751.569	100000	100000	25
16	16092.593	100000	100000	25
17	13863.2	100000	100000	25
18	22010.334	100000	93382.2	25
19	22956.245	93382.2	93382.2	23.34555
20	21905.081	93382.2	93382.2	23.34555
21	20999.067	93382.2	93382.2	23.34555
22	22681.432	93382.2	93382.2	23.34555

Step 1: In B2:B5 and B8 enter problem parameters.

Step 2: In B6 and B7 enter trial values of the Upper Limit and Target.

Step 3: In C10 we determine if we need to invest more money on Day 1. This occurs if our cash exceeds the upper limit T:

$$= IF(B10>=\$B\$6,"yes","no").$$

Step 4: **In D10 we determine on Day 1 if we need to sell securities.** We sell securities if our cash level is below the minimum value:

$$= IF(B10 <= \$B\$5,"yes","no").$$

Step 5: **In E10 we record the transaction cost (if any) for Day 1:**

$$=IF(OR(C10="yes",D10="yes"),\$B\$2,0).$$

Step 6: **In F10 we determine our random cash inflow for Day 1 with the formula**

$$=RiskNormal(\$B\$3,\$B\$4).$$

Step 7: **In G10 we determine the change in cash from our Day 1 transactions with the formula**

$$=IF(C10="yes",-(B10-\$B\$7),IF(D10="yes",(\$B\$7-B10),0)).$$

If we need to invest more money, we decrease our cash position by B10-B7. If we need to sell securities we increase our cash position by B7 - B10.

Step 8: **In cell H10 we compute our ending Day 1 cash balance by adding to our beginning Day 1 balance Day 1 cash inflows and changes due to Day 1 transactions:**

$$=B10+F10+G10.$$

Step 9: **In cell I10 we enter our beginning security balance.**

Step 10 : **In cell J10 we determine our ending security balance by adding the net effect of Day 1 transactions to our initial security balance:**

$$=I10-G10.$$

Step 11: **In cell K10 we compute our Day 1 interest.** We assume interest is received on the beginning Securities Balance.

$$=\$B\$8*I10.$$

Step 12: **In cell B11 we compute our beginning Day 2 balance by adding Day 1 interest to the Day 1 ending balance.**

$$=H10+K10.$$

Step 13: **In cell I11 we compute our beginning Day 2 Security balance with the formula**

$=J10.$

Step 14: In all other columns we simply copy the Row 10 formula to Row 11.

Step 15: We now generate 98 more days of the simulation by copying B11:K11 to B12:K100.

Step 16: In F7 we compute our total profit for the 100 days by finding total interest and subtracting total transactions costs with the formula

$=SUM(K10:K110)-SUM(E10:E110).$

Step 17: We are now ready to use RISKOptimizer to determine a target T and upper value U that maximize expected profit. Our Model window follows:

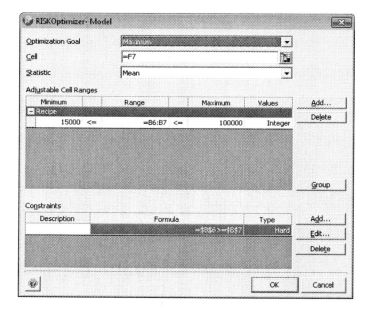

We choose to maximize mean profit (F7). Our adjustable cells are our target (B7) and Upper Limit (B6). We constrain our Target and Upper Limit to be integers between $15,000 and $100,000. Of course, the simulation constraint B6>=B7 ensures that our Upper Limit is not less than the target.

From Figure 18.1 we find maximum mean profit is $2021 (around $20 per day). We obtain this profit with a Target of $28,063 and Upper Limit of $65,592. Thus if at beginning of day we have less than $15,000 cash, we transfer enough out of securities to bring cash up to $28,063. If at beginning of day we have at least $65,592 in cash, we transfer enough into securities to reduce our beginning cash to $28,063.

Remark

Instead of defining a minimum balance, we could have made the Minimum Balance an adjustable cell. If we then assess a cost each time ending cash dips below a certain amount, RISKOptimizer could determine a minimum level for cash (M) such that if beginning cash is below M we transfer enough from securities to cash to bring our beginning cash level to T.

Reference

Miller, M., and Orr, D., "A Model for the Demand of Money by Firms, *Quarterly Journal of Economics,* Volume 80 No. 8 (1966), pages 413-435.

Chapter 19: Using RISKOptimizer and Solver to Determine Optimal Plant Capacities

Consider the problem of determining the optimal configuration of plant capacities for a new product. We do not know the demand for the product, so determination of optimal capacity levels is difficult. Once we set a capacity level, we know we will optimize distribution given those capacity levels. To begin we need to be able to compute mean profit for a given set of plant capacities. This requires that we have RISKOptimizer generate a set of random demands for each customer. For each set of random demands we use the Excel Solver to determine the profit maximizing distribution strategy. Then we make RISKOptimizer choose capacity levels at each plant as adjustable cells to maximize mean profit. Our analysis requires us to run a macro (which embeds our Solver model) after each demand sample is generated. Here is an example of how to set up this type of problem:

Example 19.1   We produce a drug at LA, NY and INDY. We sell the drug to customers in the East, South, Southwest, Midwest and West. The profit (in $s) earned on a unit of each drug depends on the plant and region as follows (see Figure 19.1 and file Solverdrug.xls):

Figure 19.1

	C	D	E	F	G	H
1	**Profits**					
2		East	South	SW	MW	West
3	LA	1	2.2	2.6	3	4
4	Indy	1.5	3.2	3	5	2.8
5	NY	3	2.9	2.6	3.8	2.6

It costs $1.50 to maintain a unit of production capacity for a year. The annual demand in each region is unknown but assumed to be normally distributed with the following mean and standard deviations (see Figure 19.2):

Figure 19.2

	C	D	E	F	G	H
16	Actual Demands	370.5889207	377.4219	351.3637	518.683	475.4647
17	Mean	400	300	400	500	380
18	Std Dev	100	80	90	100	100

We would like to determine the combination of capacities that maximizes our expected profit.

Solution

Our work is in Figure 19.3.

Step by Step

Step 1: We first enter trial demands in D14:H14 and enter trial shipments in D9:H11.

Step 2: Next we compute the total produced at each plant in I9:I11. We can do this with the summation icon.

Step 3: Next we use the summation icon to compute the total amount sold in each region in D12:H12.

Step 4: In A7 we compute total profit with the formula

$$=SUMPRODUCT(D3:H5,D9:H11) - 1.5*SUM(K9:K11).$$

Step 5: **Now we set up a Solver model to maximize our annual profit for the given set of trial demands.** The Solver Parameters window is as follows:

Figure 19.3

	A	B	C	D	E	F	G	H	I	J	K
1			Profits								
2				East	South	SW	MW	West			
3			LA	1	2.2	2.6	3	4			
4			Indy	1.5	3.2	3	5	2.8			
5			NY	3	2.9	2.6	3.8	2.6			
6	Total Profit										
7	4518.7055										
8			Shipped	East	South	SW	MW	West	Produced		Capacity
9			LA	0	0	0	0	404.98	404.9774	<=	600
10	Mean =		Indy	0	391.14	378.978	435.738	0	1205.852	<=	700
11	4142.92		NY	416.35	0	0	0	0	416.3452	<=	645
12			Sold	416.35	391.14	378.978	435.738	404.98			
13				<=	<=	<=	<=	<=			
14			Demand	416.35	391.14	378.978	435.738	404.98			

We simply maximize profit (A7) subject to shipping less from each plant than capacity (I9:I11<=K9:K11) and shipping less to each region than people are willing to buy (D12:H12<=D14:H14). The last set of constraints makes sure everything that is produced is sold. Run the Solver at least once before going on to the next section. Since our constraints and target cells are linear functions of our changing cells, we check the Linear Models box under Options. We also must check the box that makes all changing cells non-negative.

Setting Up a Macro to Combine Solver and RISKOptimizer Sampling

Before recording the macro generate trial demands in D16:H16 by entering the formula

$$=RiskNormal(D17, D18)$$

in cell D16 and copy it across to E16:H16.

We now go to the **View** ribbon tab, and select **Macros > Record Macro** (call it Macro1). Our macro will involve the following:

Step by Step

Step 1: Select cells D16:H16, go to the Home ribbon tab and click the Copy button.

Step 2: Click on Paste > Paste Values to paste the values to D14:H14.

Step 3: Run the Solver and click OK to keep solution.

Step 4: Go back to the View ribbon tab, and select Macros > Stop Recording to terminate the macro.

Before this macro will run you need to edit the macro, select **Tools > References** in the VBA editor, and add in the Solver. You will also need to edit the macro and change SolverSOLVE to SolverSOLVE(TRUE). The macro will now look like this:

```
Range("D16:H16").Select
  Selection.Copy
  Range("D14").Select
  Selection.PasteSpecial Paste:=xlValues, Operation:=xlNone, SkipBlanks:= _
      False, Transpose:=False
  SolverOk SetCell:="$A$7", MaxMinVal:=1, ValueOf:="0",
ByChange:="$D$9:$H$11"
  SolverSolve (True)
End Sub
```

This macro generates a set of random demand for each customer and then determines (for the given levels of capacity) a profit maximizing distribution strategy.

Using RISKOptimizer to Find Optimal Plant Capacities

We now choose to maximize mean profit (A7) by adjusting plant capacities (cells K9:K11). We constrain each plant capacity to be an integer between 0 and 2000.

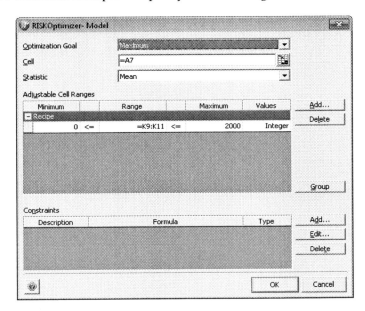

We need to ensure that our macro is run after each recalculation of the spreadsheet. To do this, click the Settings button on the RISKOptimizer ribbon tab, select Macros and fill in the dialog box as follows:

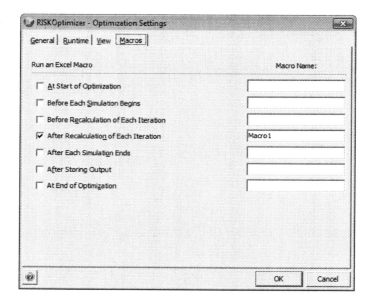

Each "iteration" of a simulation involves a Solver model and is time-consuming. Therefore we reduced number of iterations to 30 (probably too small, but I have a slow computer!). From Figure 19.3 we find that (after 12 hours) RISKOptimizer found a maximum mean profit of $4142. This maximum mean profit was obtained by an annual capacity of 600 in LA, 700 in Indianapolis, and 645 in New York. Note that mean annual demand is 1980 and RISKOptimizer chose a total capacity of 1945. This is because the high fixed cost of capacity makes us not want to incur the risk of building a unit of capacity that has a high chance of being unused.

Chapter 20: Modeling Managerial Flexibility

Many manufacturing companies are trying to decide whether they should invest in more flexible machinery. We describe the degree of flexibility of a machine by the number of products the machine can make. A more flexible machine usually costs more money, but if you have flexible machines you are less vulnerable to demand uncertainty. This is because the flexible machine can "pick up the slack" if demand for one product is unexpectedly high and demand for another product is unexpectedly low. The following example shows how to combine RISKOptimizer and Solver to determine the optimal mix of flexible and inflexible machinery.

Example 20.1 HN Auto produces two cars: A and B. Each car sells for $10,000. HN is trying to determine the optimal capacity configuration. They have the following options for machinery investment:

- They can invest in machinery (a type A machine) that can just produce type A cars. This incurs a building cost of $4000 per unit of annual capacity. It costs $4000 to build a type A car on a type A machine.

- HN can also invest in machinery (a type B machine) that can produce just type B cars. For a type B machine it costs $5000 to build a unit of annual capacity. It costs $5000 to produce a type B car on a type B machine.

- Finally, HN can build a unit of flexible machinery (type AB) that can produce *either* a type A or type B car. For a type AB machine it costs $7000 to build a unit of annual capacity. It costs $5500 to produce either type of car on a type AB Machine.

During year 1 HN knows that demand for type A cars will equal 50,000 and demand for type B cars will equal 60,000. In later years the annual growth in demand is uncertain. Each year the worst case growth in type A demand is a drop of 70%, most likely is demand will increase by 10%, and best case is demand will double. Each year the worst case growth in type B demand is a drop of 50%, most likely is demand will increase by 0%, and best case is demand will increase by 60%. If our goal is to maximize expected NPV earned from five years of sales, how much of each type of capacity should be built? Assume a discount rate of 10%.

Solution

As in Chapter 19, we need to combine RISKOptimizer and Solver. We input trial values of capacity and generate random demands for Years 1-5. Using a macro we use copy and paste special values for these demands and run a Solver model which determines, for the trial values of capacity and one set of random demands, the production strategy that maximizes NPV. Then we generate another set of random demands and again use Solver to maximize NPV. After enough iterations, we have a good idea of the mean NPV for our trial values of capacity. Then RISKOptimizer tries another trial set of capacities. Eventually, RISKOptimizer zeroes in on a set of capacities that comes close to maximizing mean NPV.

Here's how things go: Our work is in Figure 20.1 and file flex.xls.

Figure 20.1

	A	B	C	D	E
4		BC	UPC	Price	Capacity
5	A	$ 4.00	$ 4.00	$ 10.00	31719
6	B	$ 5.00	$ 5.00	$ 10.00	25000
7	Flexible	$ 7.00	$ 5.50		35827

	A	B	C	D	E	F	G
10	Year	0	1	2	3	4	5
11	A Demand risk		50000	39718.23666	39608.68121	46823.04294	41584.01353
12	B Demand Risk		60000	54256.75112	68425.00936	87249.8113	76200.59913
13	A A		31719	31719	31719	31719	31719
14	AF		18281	6029.213239	7212.03446	35827	35827
15	BB		38678	38678	38678	38678	38678
16	BF		17546	29797.78676	28614.96554	0	0
17	Copied A Demand		50000	61098.56147	60547.72831	47784.73186	62903.46629
18	Copied B demand		60000	63060.26382	56737.21891	66892.15397	77238.33367
19	AA+AF		50000	37748.21324	38931.03446	67546	67546
20			<=	<=	<=	<=	<=
21	Demand A		50000	61098.56147	60547.72831	47784.73186	62903.46629
22							
23	BB+BF		56224	68475.78676	67292.96554	38678	38678
24			<=	<=	<=	<=	<=
25	Demand B		60000	63060.26382	56737.21891	66892.15397	77238.33367
26							
27	AF+BF		35827	35827	35827	35827	35827
28			<=	<=	<=	<=	<=
29	Flex capacity		35827	35827	35827	35827	35827
30	A revenue		$ 500,000.00	$ 377,482.13	$ 389,310.34	$ 675,460.00	$ 675,460.00
31	B revenue		$ 562,240.00	$ 684,757.87	$ 672,929.66	$ 386,780.00	$ 386,780.00
32	Building cost	$ 502,665.00					
33	AA cost		$ 126,876.00	$ 126,876.00	$ 126,876.00	$ 126,876.00	$ 126,876.00
34	AF cost		$ 100,545.50	$ 33,160.67	$ 39,666.19	$ 197,048.50	$ 197,048.50
35	BB Cost		$ 193,390.00	$ 193,390.00	$ 193,390.00	$ 193,390.00	$ 193,390.00
36	BF cost		$ 96,503.00	$ 163,887.83	$ 157,382.31	$ -	$ -
37	Profit	$ (502,665.00)	$ 544,925.50	$ 544,925.50	$ 544,925.50	$ 544,925.50	$ 544,925.50
38							
39	NPV	$1,563,031.38					
40							
41							
42				Mean = 765508.6118			
43							

Step by Step   **Step 1: In C17:G18 generate the random demand for each type of car.** For Year 1 demand is not random so we enter actual demand in cells C11 and C12. In D11:G11 we generate random demands for type A cars in Years 2-5 by copying the formula

=C11*RiskTriang(0.3,1.1,2)

from D11 to E11:G11.

In D12:G12 we generate the random demand for type B cars by copying the formula

=C12*RiskTriang(0.5,1,1.6)

from D12 to E12:G12.

Also enter trial values of type A, type B, and flexible capacity in cells E5:E7.

Step 2: In C13:G16 we enter trial values for the number of cars of each type produced on each type of machine during each year.

AA= Type A cars produced on Type A machine
BB = Type B cars produced on Type B machine.
AF = Type A cars produced on flexible machine.
BF = Type B cars produced on flexible machine.

Step 3: In rows 17-29 we set up constraints for a Solver model that will be used to determine for a given set of random demands the production plan that maximizes NPV.

Step 4: In rows 17 and 18 enter arbitrary values for Years 1-5 demands of each product. Our Macro will later paste in random demands generated by RISKOptimizer.

Step 5: In rows 19-21 we set up constraints which ensure that during each year we make no more A than is demanded. In C19:G19 we compute amount of A made each year by copying from C19 to D19:G19 the formula

=C13+C14.

Step 6: In C21:G21 we recopy the demand generated by RISKOptimizer by copying from C21 to D21:G21 the formula

=C17.

Step 7: In C23:G25 we set up (in a similar fashion to Steps 5 and 6) constraints which ensure that during each year we make no more B than is demanded.

Step 8: In rows 27-29 we set up constraints which ensure that the number of cars built each year with flexible capacity does not exceed our flexible capacity. In C27:G27 we compute the number of cars built with flexible capacity each year by copying from C27 to D27:G27 the formula

$=C14+C16.$

Step 9: In C29: G29 we compute the amount of flexible capacity available each year by copying the formula

$=\$E\$7$

from C29 to D29:G29. Note: Trial values of capacity have been entered in E5:E7.

Step 10: In rows 30-37 we compute our annual costs and revenues. In C30:G30 we compute annual revenues from type A cars by multiplying type A cars produced each year times sales price. To do this copy from C30 to D30:G30 the formula

$=C19*\$D\$5.$

In a similar fashion we compute the revenue from Type B cars in C31:G31. Since total produced is constrained to not exceed total demand, we know that all cars produced will be sold.

Step 11: In rows 33-36 we compute the cost of each type of production during each year. For example, in C36:G36 we compute the annual cost of producing type B cars on the flexible machine by copying the formula

$=C16*\$C\$7$

from C36 to D36:G36.

Step 12: In B32 we compute our cost (assumed incurred in Year 0) of building capacity with the formula

$=SUMPRODUCT(B5:B7,E5:E7).$

Step 13: In B37:G37 we compute profit for each year. For Year 0 profit is just -(building cost). For Years 1-5 compute annual profit in C37:G37 by copying from C37 to D37:G37 the formula

$=C30+C31-C33-C34-C35-C36.$

Step 14: In B39 compute NPV for years 0-5. Assuming all cash flows are at beginning of year this NPV is given by

$$=B37+NPV(0.1,C37:G37).$$

Step 15: We can now set up a Solver model that (for a given set of capacities and random demand) determines a production schedule that maximizes NPV. Our Solver window follows:

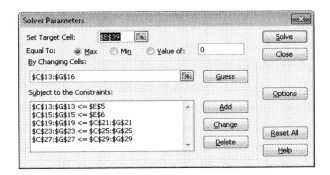

We choose to maximize NPV (cell B39) by adjusting each year's production of cars on each type of machine (cells C13:G16). All changing cells must be nonnegative. The constraints C13:G13<=E5 ensure that during each year we do not produce more type A cars on type A machines than capacity available. Similarly the constraints C15:G15<=E6 ensure that during each year we do not produce more type B cars on type B machine than capacity available. The constraints C19:G19<=C21:G21 ensure we do not produce more type A cars in a year than we can sell. Similarly, the constraints C23:G23<=C25:G25 ensure that we do not produce more type B cars in a year than we can sell. Finally, the constraints C27:G27<=C29:G29 ensure that number of cars produced each year with flexible capacity does not exceed available capacity. Since our constraints and target cells are linear functions of our changing cells, we check the Linear Model box under Options. We must also check the non-negative changing cells box.

Setting Up the Macro

We now set up the Macro needed to generate random demands and solve for the NPV maximizing production plan.

Step by Step **Step 1: Go to the View ribbon tab, select Macros > Record New Macro, and name the macro solvercap.**

Step 2: Select the cells C11:G12 and copy them to the clipboard.

Step 3: Select Paste > Paste Values on the Home ribbon tab to paste the cell values in the cells C17:G18.

Step 4: Go to the Data ribbon tab, select Solver and run the solver model.

As described in Chapter 19, you must make some changes before this macro will run. While editing the macro select **Tools > Reference** and add in the Solver. You will also need to edit macro and change **SolverSolve** to **SolverSolve(TRUE)**. The macro will now look as follows:

```
Sub solvercap()
'
' solvercap Macro
' Macro recorded 11/28/98 by wayne winston
'

'
  Range("C11:G12").Select
  Selection.Copy
  Range("C17").Select
  Selection.PasteSpecial Paste:=xlValues, Operation:=xlNone, SkipBlanks:= _
    False, Transpose:=False
  SolverOk SetCell:="$B$39", MaxMinVal:=1, ValueOf:="0",
ByChange:="$C$13:$G$16"
  SolverSolve (True)
End Sub.
```

Using RISKOptimizer to find the Optimal Capacities

We are now ready to use RISKOptimizer to determine the set of capacities that maximize expected NPV. Our Model window follows:

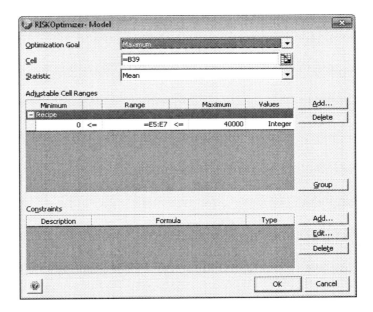

We choose to maximize mean NPV (E39) by adjusting capacities (E5:E7). We constrain these capacities to be integers between 0 and 40,000.

We click the Settings button on the RISKOptimizer ribbon tab, select Macros and fill in the dialog box as follows:

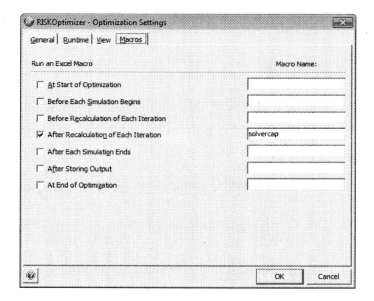

This ensures that for each set of capacities a random set of demands will be generated, and then an NPV maximizing production schedule will be found. After several hours RISKOptimizer found the solution in Figure 20.1 which recommends 31,719 units of type A capacity, 25,070 units of type B capacity, and 35,827 units of flexible capacity. A mean NPV of $766,000 is obtained.

Chapter 21: Capacity Planning for an Electric Utility

In this era of deregulation, power companies have many complex decisions to make. For example, should a power company sell some of their power plants and buy power from other producers? The problem with this is that on hot days when power usage is high it can be very expensive to purchase power. If we choose to never purchase power from other producers, however, we incur high daily fixed costs for operating our plants. The following example shows how RISKOptimizer and Solver can be used to determine which power plants a power company should be operating and which should be closed.

Example 21.1 Power Company PSI currently operates four power plants. Figure 21.1 gives daily capacity (in 000's of kWh) and cost information for each plant. See file Electric.xls.

Figure 21.1

	A	B	C	D	E
4	Open	1	1	0	0
5	Plants	1	2	3	4
6	Fixed cost/day	110	220	280	320
7	var cost/kwh(000)	4.3	4.2	4.5	4
8	capacity	60	70	50	80

For example, Plant 1 can produce 60,000 kWh per day. It costs $4.30 to produce 1000 kWh at Plant 1. Also, the fixed cost per day of operating Plant 1 is $110.

Daily demand for power is highly uncertain. There are three types of days: high demand, medium demand and low demand. The probability of each type of day occurring and the mean and standard deviation of demand (in '000s of kWh's) for each type of day are given in Figure 21.2.

Figure 21.2

	A	B	C	D	E	F
10	Type of Day	Code	Prob	Mean	Sigma	Cost/kwh(000)
11	High	1	0.2	200	40	15
12	Medium	2	0.6	100	20	10
13	Low	3	0.2	50	10	5

For example, there is a 20% chance of a high demand day, a 60% chance of a medium demand day, and a 20% chance of a low demand day. On a high demand day mean demand is for 200,000 kWh and standard deviation is 40,000 kWh. The cost of buying 1000 kWh on each type of day is also given. For example, on a high demand day it costs $15 to buy 1,000 kWh. Which plants should PSI keep open?

Solution

Our Adjustable Cell Ranges for RISKOptimizer will be 0-1 cells for each plant. A "1" will mean the plant is open and a "0" means the plant is closed. The target for RISKOptimizer will be to minimize mean daily cost. We will use RISKOptimizer to generate the type of day and the actual kWh demand for the day. Then a Solver model will be solved to minimize the non-fixed cost (purchase + variable plant cost) for the day. Averaging the solutions to many of these Solver problems will give us an estimate of the mean daily cost of providing power for the current plant configuration. Then another plant configuration will be tried. Eventually, RISKOptimizer finds the plant configuration that minimizes mean daily cost. See Figure 21.3

Figure 21.3

	A	B	C	D	E	F
14						
15	Actual day	3	mean	sigma		
16	Actual demand	60.77375	50	10		
17		1	2	3	4	
18	Produced	0	12.02767282	0	80	
19		<=	<=	<=	<=	
20	logical capacity	60	70	0	0	
21						
22						
23	Bought	0		**Pasted**		
24				actual day	demand	
25	Produced+Bought	92.02767	=	2	92.02767	
26						
27	**Cost**					
28	Fixed cost/day	330				
29	variable cost/day	370.5162	unit cost/day			
30	purchase cost/day	0	10			
31	vc/day	370.5162				
32						
33	total cost/day	700.5162				

Step 1: Enter trial values (0 or 1) in B4:E4 for each plant. A "1" indicates the plant is in operation and a "0" indicates that a plant is not open. Note we either have a plant available for the whole year or none of the year; keeping a plant open on only high demand days is not an option!

Step 2: In B15:D16 we generate the type of day and actual demand. The type of day is generated in B15 with the formula

$=RiskDiscrete(B11:B13,C11:C13)$.

In C16 and D16 we compute the mean and standard deviation of the demand for the day with the formulas

$=VLOOKUP(\$B\$15,\$B\$11:\$E\$13,3)$ and $=VLOOKUP(\$B\$15,\$B\$11:\$E\$13,4)$,

respectively.

In B16 we compute actual demand with the formula

$=RiskNormal(C16,D16)$.

We are assuming normal demand.

Step 3: In cell D25 and E25 we will have our macro paste the actual type of day and actual demand. We can now set up a Solver model that computes for PSI the optimal production and purchase of power for the actual demand.

Setting Up the Solver Model

Step 1: In B18:E18 enter trial values of the kWh (in '000s) produced at each plant. In B23 enter a trial value for the kWh (in '000s) purchased externally.

Step 2: Compute the maximum amount (logical capacity) that can be produced in a day at each plant in B20:E20 by copying the formula

   $=B8*B4$

from B20 to C20:E20. These formulas yield the plant capacity for each open plant and 0 for closed plants. Our Solver model will ensure that the amount produced at each plant does not exceed the logical capacity.

Step 3: In B25 compute total power produced and purchased with the formula

   $=SUM(B18:E18)+B23.$

Our Solver model will ensure this equals power demanded.

Step 4: B28:C33 compute the total operating cost for the day. In B28 we compute the fixed cost of operating the open plants with the formula

   $=SUMPRODUCT(B4:E4,B6:E6).$

Step 5: In B29 compute the variable cost of plant operation with the formula

   $=SUMPRODUCT(B18:E18,B7:E7).$

Step 6: In C30 compute today's cost of purchasing 1000 kWh with the formula

   $=VLOOKUP(D25,\$B\$11:\$F\$13,5).$

Then we compute in B30 the total cost of purchasing kWh for the day with the formula

   $=B23*C30.$

Step 7: In B31 we compute the total non-fixed cost for the day with the formula

   $=SUM(B29:B30).$

Step 8: In B33 we compute fixed and variable operating costs with the formula

   $=B28 + B31.$

Solver Model   We now set up a Solver model that will choose the amount of power produced at each plant and purchased to minimize the day's non-fixed cost. Our Solver window follows:

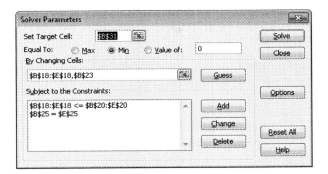

We minimize total non-fixed costs (B31) by changing production at each plant (B18:E18) and power purchased (B23). We make sure that power produced at each plant does not exceed power available (B18:E18<=B20:E20). The constraint B25=E25 ensures that power produced plus power purchased equals demand for power. All changing cells are non-negative. Since all constraints and the target cell are linear functions of the changing cells we check the *Linear Model* box under *Options*.

Setting Up the Macro

We now set up a macro (Macro4) that will generate the type of day (high, medium, or low demand) and actual demand. Then these quantities will be pasted to D25:E25. Next our Solver model will be used to determine a production and purchase plan that minimizes the day's variable costs.

Step by Step

Step 1: Select the cells B15 and B16, copy them to the clipboard, and then select Paste > Transpose on the Home ribbon tab to paste them in D25:E25.

Step 2: Run the Solver model. As described in Chapter 19, you must make some changes before this macro will run. While editing the macro select Tools > References and add in the Solver. You will also need to edit macro and change **SolverSolve** to **SolverSolve(TRUE)**. The macro will now look as follows:

```
Sub Macro4()
'
' Macro4 Macro
' Macro recorded 11/25/98 by wayne winston
'

    Range("B15:B16").Select
    Selection.Copy
    Range("D25").Select
    Selection.PasteSpecial Paste:=xlValues, Operation:=xlNone, SkipBlanks:= _
        False, Transpose:=True
    SolverOk SetCell:="$B$31", MaxMinVal:=2, ValueOf:="0", ByChange:= _
        "$B$18:$E$18,$B$23"
Solversolve (True)

End Sub
```

Using RISKOptimizer to find Optimal Plant Configuration

We are now ready to use RISKOptimizer to determine the plant configuration that minimizes expected daily cost. Our Model window follows:

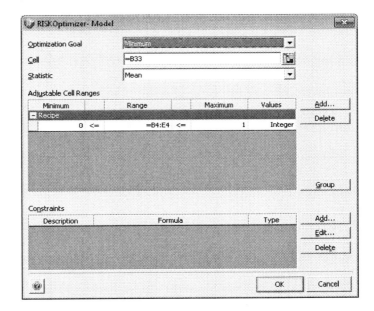

We choose to minimize mean daily cost (B33). Our adjustable cells are 0-1 cells for each plant that tell us which plants are operated (B4:E4).

We need to make sure Macro4 is run after each recalc.

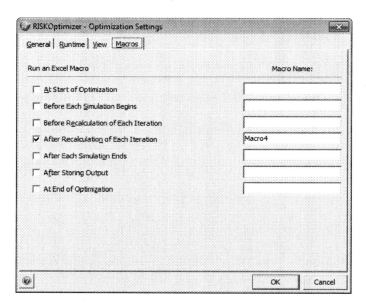

We find a minimum mean cost of $935 per day is obtained by keeping Plants 1 and 2 open and closing Plants 3 and 4.

Chapter 22: Retirement Planning

The January 11, 1999 issue of *Fortune Magazine* advocated using Monte Carlo simulation to evaluate various investment strategies for retirement. For example, if we put $1000 into a retirement fund each year for 40 years what mix of investments in bonds, T-bills and stocks would be best? How does the length of our planning horizon influence the optimal investment strategy? To answer these questions we will assume that future returns on stocks, T-bills , bonds, and future inflation will follow patterns similar to the past 70 years. We will model the returns (and annual inflation) on a person's retirement portfolio each year as a *randomly drawn scenario* from the returns for the years 1926-1994. Here's how things work:

Example 22.1   Attorney Amanda McBeal is saving for retirement. At the beginning of each of the next 40 years she will put $1000 into a retirement account. Each year she plans to allocate the same percentage to T-bills, bonds and stocks. What asset allocation will maximize the expected value of assets (in today's dollars) 40 years from now?

Solution   Our work is shown in Figures 22.1 and 22.2. (see file retiremean40.xls).

Figure 22.1

	A	B	C	D	E
3	Year	Bills	Bonds	Stocks	Inflation
4	1926	3.27	7.77	11.62	-1.49
5	1927	3.12	8.93	37.49	-2.08
6	1928	3.24	0.1	43.61	-0.97
7	1929	4.75	3.42	-8.42	0.19
8	1930	2.41	4.66	-24.9	-6.03
9	1931	1.07	-5.31	-43.34	-9.52
10	1932	0.96	16.84	-8.19	-10.3
11	1933	0.3	-0.08	53.99	0.51
12	1934	0.16	10.02	-1.44	2.03
13	1935	0.17	4.98	47.67	2.99
14	1936	0.18	7.51	33.92	1.21
15	1937	0.31	0.23	-35.03	3.1
16	1938	-0.02	5.53	31.12	-2.78
17	1939	0.02	5.94	-0.41	-0.48
18	1940	0	6.09	-9.78	0.96
19	1941	0.06	0.93	-11.59	9.72
20	1942	0.27	3.22	20.34	9.29
21	1943	0.35	2.08	25.9	3.16
22	1944	0.33	2.81	19.75	2.11

Figure 22.1 shows annual returns and inflation during the years 1926-1944 (we will use 1926-1994 in our analysis). For example, in 1926 T-bills yielded 3.27%, bonds yielded 7.77%, stocks yielded 11.62% and prices went down by 1.49%. We name the range (A4:E72) containing the asset returns and inflation for 1926-1994 Lookup.

We now simulate Amanda's 40 years of investment. Each year we use the =*RiskDuniform* function to randomly choose a year from 1926-1994 as our scenario. Then we keep track of how the value of Amanda's portfolio has changed. Finally, we keep track of inflation each year and convert Amanda's final cash position into today's dollars.

Figure 22.2

	G	H	I	J	K	L	M	N	O	P	Q
1			2	3	4	5					
2	Allocation		0.0787	0.01617	0.905			Value at retirement (today's dollars)	252.0236		
3	Beginning cash	Scenario	Bills	Bonds	Stocks	Inflation	Ending cash	Deflation		Mean = 221.0988	
4	1	1969	6.58	-5.08	-8.5	6.11	0.9274177	0.942418245			
5	1.927418	1970	6.53	12.1	4.01	5.49	2.0110499	0.893372116			
6	3.01105	1959	2.95	-2.26	11.96	1.5	3.3429032	0.880169572			
7	4.342903	1930	2.41	4.66	-24.9	-6.03	3.3755939	0.93664954			
8	4.375594	1982	10.54	40.35	21.41	3.87	5.2883865	0.901751747			

Step by Step **Step 1: In I2:K2 enter trial allocations of assets to T-Bills, bonds and stocks.** Make sure they add up to 100%.

Step 2: In G4 enter Amanda's beginning Year 1 cash (1). We will measure money in $000's.

Step 3: H4:H43 we randomly choose a year as scenario for each of Amanda's 40 years. To do this copy the formula

=*RiskDuniform($A$4:$A$72)*

from H4 to H5:H43.

Step 4: In I4:L43 we "lookup" for each year the return on each asset and inflation rate corresponding to the chosen scenario. Note that our approach preserves historic correlations between asset returns and inflation. In I4 look up Year 1 T-bill return with the formula

=*VLOOKUP($H4,Lookup,I$1)*.

Using the scenario chosen in H4, this formula looks in column 2 of the lookup range to find T-bill returns. Copying this formula to I4:L43 generates our 40 random years of asset returns and inflation.

Step 5: In cell M4 we compute the ending Year 1 value of Amanda's assets with the formula

$$=G4*(\$I\$2*(1+(I4/100))+\$J\$2*(1+(J4/100))+\$K\$2*(1+(K4/100))).$$

This formula takes the amount of money invested in each asset at the beginning of the year and changes its value based on the asset's return during Year 1.

Step 6: In N4 we compute the value (in today's dollars) of a dollar received at end of Year 1 with the formula

$$=1/(1+(L4/100)).$$

Step 7: In G5 we compute the cash available for Year 2 investment with the formula

$$=M4+1.$$

Step 8: We generate ending Year 2 asset value by copying the formula in M4 to M5.

Step 9: We generate in cell N5 the value (in today's dollars) of a dollar received at the end of Year 2 with the formula

$$=N4*(1/(1+(L5/100))).$$

Step 10: Copying our formulas from G5:N5 to G6:G43 determines how Amanda's portfolio does during each of the 40 years.

Step 11: In cell O2 we determine the value, in today's dollars, of Amanda's ending Year 40 asset position.

$$=M43*N43.$$

Step 12: We are now ready to use RISKOptimizer to determine the asset allocation mix which maximizes expected value (in today's dollars) of Amanda's retirement fund. Our model is defined as follows:

We choose to maximize mean value (in today's dollars) of ending Year 40 asset value (cell O2). We choose Budget as Solving Method to adjust our asset allocation. (I2:K2). The choice of the Budget method ensures that I2:K2 will always sum to the sum of the original numbers in these cells (1). We also ensure that our adjustable cells are non-negative. This precludes short selling. As shown in Figure 22.2, mean value of the retirement portfolio is obtained by investing 8% in T-bills, 2% in bonds, and 90% in stocks. This is consistent with the theory that investing in stocks is best for the long-run. Our average portfolio value in today's dollars will be around $221,000

A More Conservative Approach

Let's suppose we are paranoid about the world. We might then set our goal to maximize the 5th percentile of our ending Year 40 asset value (again in today's dollars). Just change your settings to the following (see file retireper40.xls). This corresponds to optimizing a "worst case scenario"

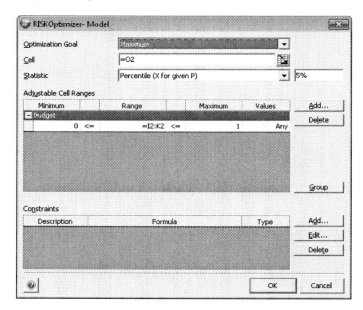

We find that the optimal asset allocation is now 8% in T-bills, 7% in bonds, and 85% in stocks. Even if we are paranoid and very risk averse, stocks still predominate. There is a 5% chance that the ending value (in today's dollars) of Amanda's portfolio will be less than $37,200.

Reducing the Length of the Planning Horizon

Is there a role for T-bills and bonds? Suppose Amanda is saving for her children's college education ten years from now. If she invests $1000 at the beginning of each year, what asset allocation will maximize the 5th percentile of her ending Year 10 asset value (in today's dollars)? To answer this question all we need to do is change our formula in cell O2 to

=M13*N13.

We find that Amanda should allocate 72% to T-bills, 9% to bonds and 19% to stocks. There is a 5% chance that the ending value of her portfolio (in today's dollars) is less than $7,740. Thus there is a role for bonds and T-bills for retirees or families with short planning horizons!

Using Utility Theory to Incorporate Risk Aversion

We have modeled the risk-averse nature of Amanda by maximizing the 5th percentile of the value of her retirement portfolio. A more traditional method for modeling risk aversion is the use of a **utility function.** A utility function associates a utility (usually between 0 and 1) with every possible outcome of an uncertain situation. Then the decision-maker simply uses RISKOptimizer to **maximize expected utility.** As we will see, the method used to construct the utility function ensures that the utility function captures the decision-maker's attitude towards risk.

We will fit an exponential utility function of the form $u(x) = ae^{-x/b} + c$. Here u(x) represents the utility Amanda "receives" if the ending value of her assets is $x (in today's dollars). The standard procedure for estimating a utility function is as follows:

1. Let the (approximately) worst outcome have a utility of 0 and the (approximately) best outcome have a utility of 1.

2. Ask the decision maker what amount (call it $x_{.5}$) makes the decision maker indifferent between the following two situations

    Situation 1: A .5 chance at best outcome and .5 chance at worst outcome.
    Situation 2: Receiving (with certainty) $x_{.5}$.

    Then $x_{.5}$ has utility .5.

3. Ask the decision maker what amount (call it $x_{.25}$) makes the decision maker indifferent between the following two situations

    Situation 1: A .5 chance at worst outcome and .5 chance at $x_{.5}$.
    Situation 2: Receiving (with certainty) $x_{.25}$.

    Then $x_{.25}$ has utility .25.

4. Ask the decision maker what amount (call it $x_{.75}$) makes the decision maker indifferent between the following two situations

    Situation 1: A .5 chance at best outcome and .5 chance at $x_{.5}$.
    Situation 2: Receiving (with certainty) $x_{.75}$.

    Then $x_{.75}$ has utility .75.

5. Now use the Excel Solver to fit a curve of the form $u(x) = ae^{-x/b} + c$ to the five points (worst outcome, 0), (best outcome, 1), $(x_{.5}, .5)$, $(x_{.75}, .75)$, $(x_{.25}, .25)$. Use the criteria of minimizing squared errors.

To determine the best and worst outcome for a 40 year horizon, we ran 1600 iterations of @RISK. We found that $3.5 million was the maximum ending value of the portfolio. The minimum ending value was around $7000. We therefore assume worst case is ending value of $0 and best case is $4 million. Next we ask Amanda what amount for certain makes her as happy as the following situation: .5 chance at $4 million and .5 chance at $0. She answers $400,000. Therefore $x_{.5}$ = $400,000. Next we ask Amanda what amount for certain makes her as happy as the following situation: .5 chance at $400,000 and .5 chance at $0. She answers $100,000. Therefore $x_{.25}$ = $100,000. Finally, we ask Amanda what amount for certain makes her as happy as the following situation: .5 chance at $400,000 and .5 chance at $4 million. She answers $1 million. Therefore $x_{.75}$ = $1 million. We now have five points on Amanda's utility curve and we may try and fit an exponential utility function to these points. Our work is in file utility.xls. See Figure 22.3.

Step by Step

Step 1: Enter 5 points on utility curve in B4:C8. We measured x in thousands of dollars.

Step 2: Enter trial values for a, b and c in C2:E2. Use INSERT NAME CREATE to create range names a, b, and c_ for C2:E2.

Step 3: In D4:D8 determine values of utility from curve $u(x) = ae^{-x/b} + c$ by copying from D4 to D5:D8 the formula

$$=a*EXP(-B4/b)+c\_.$$

Figure 22.3

	A	B	C	D	E	F	G	H
1			a	b	c			
2			-0.933026211	639.428221	0.985439			
3		Final value	Actual Utility	Fitted Utility	Sq Error			
4		0	0	0.05241305	0.002747			
5		1.00E+02	0.25	0.18749115	0.003907			
6		4.00E+02	0.5	0.48630536	0.000188			
7		1.00E+03	0.75	0.79013941	0.001611			
8		4.00E+03	1	0.98364814	0.000267			
9				SSE	0.008721			
10								
11		U(x) =a*e$^{-x/b}$+c						
12								
13					1.2			
14					1			
15					0.8		Actual Utility	
16					0.6		Fitted Utility	
17					0.4			
18					0.2			
19					0			
20								
21					0 2000 4000 6000			
22								

Step 4: In E4:E8 compute the squared error for each prediction by copying the formula

=(D4-C4)^2

from E4 to E5:E8.

Step 5: Compute sum of squared errors (SSE) in cell E9 with the formula

=SUM(E4:E8).

Step 6: Use the Excel Solver to determine values of a, b, and c which minimize SSE. Our Solver window is as follows:

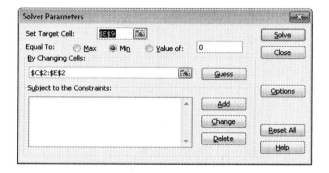

We find the best fitting exponential curve to be $u(x) = -.933e^{-x/639,42} + .985$. Note from Figure 22.3 that our utility curve is concave. This indicates a risk averse decision maker.

Using RISKOptimizer to Maximize Expected Utility

We now use RISKOptimizer to maximize expected utility of our asset value (in today's dollars) after 40 years. Our work is in file retireut.xls. See Figure 22.4. We simply compute utility of our ending asset position in cell O4 with the formula

$$=-0.933026211*EXP(-O2/639.428221)+0.985439.$$

Then we change our Target cell to maximizing mean of cell O4.

Figure 22.4

	I	J	K	L	M	N	O	P	Q
2	0.026676	0.007464	0.96586			Value at retirement (today'sdollars)	82.14337		
3	Bills	Bonds	Stocks	Inflation	Ending cash	Deflation	Utility		
4	6.35	9.67	16.81	4.42	1.164776772	0.957670944	0.164893		
5	1.2	0.06	31.71	5.79	2.828494802	0.905256588			
6	1.57	-1.3	31.56	0.37	4.996749396	0.901919486			
7	3.93	0.73	12.45	1.92	6.724469536	0.884928852		Mean = .3031	
8	4.75	3.42	-8.42	0.19	7.108033322	0.883250675			

We find that even with the risk-averse utility function graphed in Figure 22.3, Amanda should put 3% in T-bills, 1% in bonds, and 96% in stocks!

Reference
Greer, C., "Factoring Uncertainty into Retirement Planning: The Monte Carlo Method", *Fortune Magazine*, January 11, 1999.

Chapter 23: Machine Replacement Models

Many companies have to decide whether to replace a machine before it fails. A common strategy is a planned replacement interval. That is, replace every machine that has not failed after M hours of operation with a new machine. The rationale is that after a while a machine is likely to fail, and if we have not replaced it our production process will be subject to more down time than if we had made a planned replacement. Too small a value of M will result in prohibitively high replacement costs while too large a value of M will result in excessive down time. RISKOptimizer can easily be used to determine optimal planned replacement strategies.

In order to use RISKOptimizer to analyze machine replacement decisions, we need to have a distribution to model the lifetime of a machine. The Weibull distribution is the most widely used distribution for modeling the life of a machine. The Weibull distribution is specified by two parameters, α and β. If $\beta < 1$, the machine's lifetime has the decreasing failure rate property. This means that the longer the machine has operated, the less likely it is to fail during the next few seconds. If $\beta > 1$, the machine's lifetime has the increasing failure rate property. This means that the longer the machine has operated, the more likely it is to fail during the next few seconds. If $\beta = 1$, then the machine's lifetime is exponential and has the constant failure rate or lack of memory property. The lack of memory property implies that no matter how long a machine has been operating, its chance of failing during the next few seconds remains the same.

To generate a machine lifetime with @RISK or RISKOptimizer from a Weibull distribution with given parameters α and β enter the statement

$$= RiskWeibull(\alpha, \beta).$$

Given the mean and variance of a machine's lifetime, the file Weibest.xls (see Figure 23.1) enables you to estimate α and β for the machine's lifetime. Simply enter the mean lifetime of the machine in cell D4 and the variance of the machine's lifetime in cell D5. Then the values of α and β can be read in cells G7 and G8. For example, if the mean lifetime of a machine is 46,000 hours and the variance of its lifetime is 156,000,000 hours, then we estimate that $\alpha = 4.2$ and $\beta = 50,608.5$.

Figure 23.1

	A	B	C	D	E	F	G
1		**Estimating Weibull**					
2		**Distribution Parameters**					
3							
4		Mean time to failure		46000			
5		Variance of time to Failure		1.56E+08			
6		Second Moment of failure time		2.27E+09			
7		Second moment/(mean)^2		1.073842		Beta	50608.53
8		Alpha				Alpha	4.2

The following example shows how to use the Weibull distribution to analyze equipment replacement decisions.

Example 23.1   The lifetime of a stamping press used to manufacture truck bodies follows a Weibull distribution with $\alpha = 6$ and $\beta = 60$. Every hour the drill press is down costs the plant \$200. It costs \$5000 to purchase a new drill press. If we make a planned replacement of a drill press, the press will be down for 2 hours; if we need to replace a failed drill press, the press will be down for 20 hours. We are considering introducing a strategy of letting a drill press run for a specified number of hours, and then replacing it. What strategy will minimize our expected cost per hour?

Solution   Our spreadsheet is in Figure 23.2 (see file Weibull.xls). To model a given replacement strategy we will simulate the operation of the drill press for a substantial length of time (say 1000 hours) and determine a planned replacement strategy that minimizes estimated expected costs (downtime and replacement) of operating a press for 1000 hours. We proceed as follows:

Figure 23.2

	A	B	C	D	E	F	G	H
1	Determining optimal							
2	replacement policy							
3								
4	Cost per hour of down time		$ 200.00					
5	Cost of replacement		$ 5,000.00					
6	Hours for planned replacement		2					
7	Hours for unplanned replacement		20					
8	Weibull alpha		6					
9	Weibull beta		60					Total cost
10	Planned replacement interval		54	Totals		90000	18000	108000
11					Down-Time	Replacement	Down-time	
12	Time	Next Failure	Next planned replacement	Over?	Hours	Cost	Cost	
13	0	64.59402332	54	1	2	5000	400	
14	56	123.488651	110	1	2	5000	400	
15	112	167.2425278	166	1	2	5000	400	
16	168	226.621591	222	1	2	5000	400	
17	224	290.5187284	278	1	2	5000	400	
18	280	327.1328211	334	1	20	5000	4000	
19	347.1328	394.5260555	401.1328211	1	20	5000	4000	
20	414.5261	473.1644981	468.5260555	1	2	5000	400	
21	470.5261	526.0095767	524.5260555	1	2	5000	400	
22	526.5261	586.6669971	580.5260555	1	2	5000	400	
23	582.5261	650.0079119	636.5260555	1	2	5000	400	
24	638.5261	696.0520801	692.5260555	1	2	5000	400	
25	694.5261	761.8473285	748.5260555	1	2	5000	400	
26	750.5261	816.9741027	804.5260555	1	2	5000	400	
27	806.5261	859.6362767	860.5260555	1	20	5000	4000	
28	879.6363	938.1555077	933.6362767	1	2	5000	400	

Mean = 118374

Step by Step

Step 1: Begin at Time 0 and determine (in columns B and C) the lifetime of the machine and the next planned replacement.

Step 2: Determine (in column D) whether the 1000-hour time limit has been exceeded. If it has, no more costs should be incurred.

Step 3: Determine the number of downtime hours associated with the replacement of the current press (column E).

Step 4: Determine the replacement of downtime cost associated with the replacement of the current press (columns F and G).

Step 5: Determine the time the next press will begin operation (column A) by the relation

(Time operation of next press begins) =   **(23.1)**
    Minimum (Time Current Press Fails, Time of Next Planned Replacement)+
    (Downtime Associated with Current Machine)

If we type the formula

    =RiskWeibull(6, 60)

in our spreadsheet, we find (if the Monte Carlo option is off) that the mean life of a machine is 55.6 hours. With this in mind, it seems reasonable to begin by experimenting with replacing the press after say, 50, hours of operation. We now proceed as follows:

Step 6: In the cell range C4:C9 we enter the inputs to our problem. In cell C10 we enter 50 as a trial replacement interval.

Step 7: Enter a 0 in cell A13 to indicate the start of the simulation.

Step 8: In cell B13 we compute the time the first drill press fails by generating the lifetime of the first press with a Weibull distribution and adding this lifetime to the time the press begins operation (0). Thus we enter in cell B13 the formula

    =A13+ RiskWeibull(C$8, C$9).

Step 9: We now compute the instant of the next planned replacement by the relationship

    (Next Planned Replacement)=
        (Time of Current Machine's Start of Operation)+
        (Planned Replacement Interval).

To do this enter in cell C13 the formula

    =A13+C$10.

Step 10: In cell D13 we determine whether 1000 hours has been exceeded (indicated by a 0) with the formula

=IF (A13<1000, 1, 0).

Step 11: In cell E13 we determine the number of downtime hours associated with the replacement of the first press with the formula

=IF (B13<=C13, C$7, C$6).

This records a downtime of 20 hours if the machine is replaced due to failure and a downtime of 2 hours if the machine is replaced due to a planned replacement.

Step 12: In cell F13 we compute the replacement cost associated with the first press with the formula

=D13*C$5.

Step 13 In cell G13 we compute the downtime cost associated with the first press with the formula

=D13*E13*C$4

This formula will pick up the downtime cost for the press only if the simulation has not yet run 1000 hours.

Step 14: In cell A14 we determine the time the second press begins operation by operationalizing (23.1) with the formula

=MIN (B13, C13) + E13

Step 15: It seems unlikely that the minimum planned replacement interval would be less than 20 hours. Therefore we will constrain the planned replacement interval to be at least 20 hours. Accounting for the 2 hours of downtime associated with each planned replacement, 1000 hours of operation would require at most $1000/22 = 46$ press replacements. Therefore we need only copy our spreadsheet down to row 59. We now copy the formula in A14 to the range A14:A59. Next we copy the formulas in the range B13:G13 to the range B14:G59.

Step 16: In cell F10 we compute the total replacement cost incurred in 1000 hours with the formula

= SUM (F13:F59).

Copying this formula to cell G10 computes the total downtime cost.

Step 17: Finally, in cell H10 we compute the total cost incurred during 1000 hours of operation with the formula

=SUM (F10: G10).

Step 18: We are now ready to use RISKOptimizer to determine the replacement interval that minimizes expected cost for 1000 hours. Our Model window is as follows:

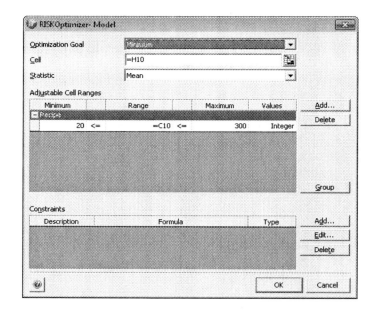

We choose to minimize expected costs for 1000 hours by adjusting the amount of time we let a press run before replacing the press. We constrain the replacement interval to be an integer between 20 and 300 hours. RISKOptimizer chose to replace the machine every 54 hours. This strategy yields an expected cost of $118,374, or around $118 per hour of operation.

Chapter 24: Using RISKOptimizer to Optimize Audit Sampling

Auditors often try to estimate the mean or variance of a population in a cost-effective manner. The only way, of course, to surely know the mean of a population is to completely sample the entire population. As shown in the following two examples, RISKOptimizer can be a very useful tool for determining cost-effective sampling plans. Before proceeding with our examples, we need to review some basic results from statistics. Let

N = Population size.
n = Sample size.
σ = Population standard deviation

- For a sample of any size, the sample mean is a random variable having a mean equal to the actual population mean and a standard deviation given by

$$\frac{\sigma * Multiplier}{\sqrt{n}} .$$

(24.1)

Here

$$Multiplier = \frac{\sqrt{N - n}}{\sqrt{N - 1}}$$

(24.2)

reduces the standard deviation of the sample mean to account for the fact that as a greater percentage of the population is sampled, the standard deviation of the sample mean must be reduced. Note that if n = N, the standard deviation of the sample mean is 0, as it should be!

- If a sample of size 30 or larger is taken, the distribution of the sample mean (or the sum of the observations) will approximately follow a normal distribution. This result holds *even if our original population is not normally distributed.* This property is known as the *Central Limit Theorem.*

We may now proceed with our examples.

Example 24.1   Big5 Auditing has been assigned to estimate the average invoice value of a population of 5000 invoices. The mean value of an invoice is unknown, but is assumed to be equally likely to be any value between $1000 and $2000. It costs $10 to analyze an invoice. If we err in estimating the true mean invoice value by $x, we assume that a cost of $10x^2$ dollars is incurred. This implies that, for example, if we are off by $5 in estimating the mean invoice size a cost of $250 is incurred. In the past invoices have had a standard deviation of $300 about the mean. What sample size minimizes the expected costs associated with the auditing procedures?

Solution   Our work is in the file sample1.xls. See Figure 24.1.

Figure 24.1

	A	B	C	D	E
1					
2	**Sample Size**				
3	Population size	5000		Error x costs	
4	Mean	1259.19		$c(x)=10x^2$	
5	Sigma	300			
6	Sample size	299			
7	Multiplier	0.969736			
8	Sample Mean	1240.571			
9	Error Cost	3466.838			
10	Sampling cost/unit	10			
11	Sampling cost	2990			
12	Total cost	6456.838			
13					
14					
15					
16				Mean = 5890.3811	

Step by Step   **Step 1: In B3 we enter the size of the population, in B5 we enter the standard deviation of invoice size, and in B10 we enter the sampling cost per invoice.**

Step 2: In B4 we generate the (random) mean invoice size with the formula

   =RiskUniform(1000,2000).

Of course, when we sample, we do not know the *actual* mean value.

Step 3: In B6 we enter a trial sample size.

Step 4: In B7 we compute the multiplier (*with formula (24.2)*) which is used in B8 to compute the standard deviation of the sample mean.

   =SQRT((B3-B6)/(B3-1)).

Step 5: In B8 we compute the actual value of the sample mean. The sample mean will be normally distributed (by the Central Limit Theorem) with a mean equal to the actual population mean and a standard deviation given by (24.1) above

$=RiskNormal(B4,B5*B7/SQRT(B6)).$

Step 6: In B9 we compute the cost incurred by our estimation error with the formula

$=10*(B4-B8)\textasciicircum2.$

Step 7: In B11 we compute our sampling cost with the formula

$=B10*B6.$

Step 8: In B12 we compute our total cost for a sample (error plus sampling cost) with the formula

$=B11+B9.$

Step 9: We are now ready to use RISKOptimizer to determine the sample size that minimizes expected cost. Our Model window is as follows:

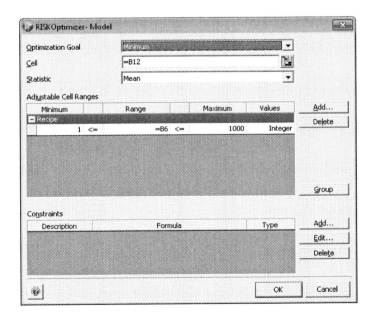

We simply minimize the mean total cost (cell B12) by adjusting the sample size (B6). We will assume our sample size can be at most 1000. From Figure 24.1 we find a sample size of 299 minimizes our expected cost per sample (at $5890). Note that RISKOptimizer chooses a sample size by setting expected estimation cost almost exactly equal to sampling cost. This is a result reminiscent of the Economic Order Quantity result in inventory.

Stratified Sampling

In many applications we can divide our population into subpopulations or *strata* that are fairly similar. Then the question becomes how many items to sample from each stratum. The following example shows how RISKOptimizer can be used to determine optimal allocations in stratified sampling.

Example 24.2 We are trying to determine, as accurately as possible, the total inventory value of 1600 items. We only have enough resources to analyze 100 items. There are basically three types of items in inventory. For each item we know the largest, smallest and most likely value for the *actual mean value* of those types of items. We also know for each type of item the standard deviation about the actual mean of items in that stratum. This data is displayed in Figure 24.2. For example, for the first type of item the mean item value is most likely to be $12,000, the mean size could be as low as $10,000 or as high as $14,000. The actual value of an item of the first type has a standard deviation of $500 about the actual mean. See the file Sampling2.xls.

Figure 24.2

	A	B	C	D	E	F	G	H	I	J	K
1			**Mean**								
2	Strata	Pop	Low	Medium	High	Act Mean	Sigma	Samp Si	Multiplier	Samp Mean	
3	1	100	10000	12000	14000	13890.8	500	64	0.603023	13849.4306	
4	2	500	400	500	700	603.03	40	24	0.976682	606.871868	
5	3	1000	80	100	130	102.959	10	12	0.994479	100.446203	
6											
7								Est Total	1788825		
8								Actual Total	1793557		
9								Abs Error	4732.12		
10											
11											
12										Mean = 4826.4496	
13											

Solution Our goal is to allocate a sample of size 100 to the three strata to minimize the expected error in estimating total inventory value.

Step by Step **Step 1: In H3:H5 enter trial values of the sample size for each strata.** Make sure they add to 100!

Step 2: In F3:F5 we compute the actual mean size of each type of item by copying from F3 to F4:F5 the formula

=RiskTriang(C3,D3,E3).

Step 3: In I3:I5 use (24.2) to compute the multiplier for each strata by copying from I3 to I4:I5 the formula

=SQRT((B3-H3)/(B3-1)).

Step 4: In J3:J5 we compute the sample mean for each type of item using (24.1), (24.2) and the Central Limit Theorem. Copy from J3 to J4:J5 the formula

=RiskNormal(F3,G3*I3/SQRT(H3)).

Step 5: In H7 we compute the estimated total value (based on sample) of our inventory. For each type of item we estimate the total value of that type of item by multiplying our estimated mean times the number of items of that type.

=SUMPRODUCT(J3:J5,B3:B5).

Step 6: In H8 we compute the *actual value* of all items by multiplying the actual mean for each item times the number of items of that type.

=SUMPRODUCT(B3:B5,F3:F5).

Step 7: In H9 we compute the absolute value of our estimation error with the formula

=ABS(H7-H8).

Step 8: We are now ready to use RISKOptimizer to determine an optimal sampling plan. Our model definition is as follows:

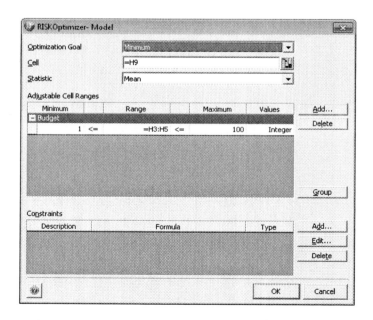

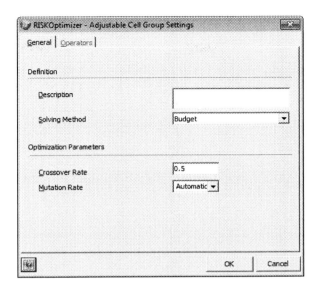

We choose to minimize average absolute estimation error (cell H9) by adjusting the sample size for each strata (H3:H5). These are integers between 1 and 100 that must add to 100. To ensure that the sample sizes add to 100 we use the BUDGET method.

From Figure 24.2 we find that 64 Type 1 items, 24 type 2 items, and 12 Type 3 items should be sampled. Our average estimation error is $4826. Note that most of our sampling effort is devoted to Type 1 items. This is because there is a high degree of uncertainty about the mean value of a Type 1 item as well as a high standard deviation of a Type 1 item's value about its mean.

Chapter 25: The Risk Neutral Approach to Option Pricing

Any investment strategy must balance expected return against risk. Options and futures are key weapons that can be used to control riskiness of investment portfolios. RISKOptimizer can be used to determine the combination of investments and derivatives (such as futures and options) which can maximize expected return subject to a constraint on the desired level of risk. In this chapter we explain the *risk neutral* approach, which enables us to use simulation to value financial derivatives. In Chapter 26 we will discuss the *Lognormal random variable* which is used to model prices of many assets, such as stocks. After defining various types of options, we give a brief discussion of the risk neutral approach to pricing derivatives. The reader is referred to Winston (1998) for further discussion of how simulation is used to model financial assets and derivatives. In later chapters we will combine these ideas with RISKOptimizer to solve many interesting financial optimization problems.

Option Definitions

A *European option* on a stock gives the owner of the option the right to buy (if the option is a *call option*) or sell (if the option is a *put option*) one share of stock for a particular price (*the exercise price*) on a particular date (the *exercise date*). An *American option* allows you buy or sell the stock at any date between the present and the exercise date.

Arbitrage Arguments and the Risk Neutral Approach

Options are usually priced by arbitrage arguments. For example, suppose 3 months from now a stock will sell for either $18 (bad state) or $22 (good state). The stock currently sells for $20 and we own a 3-month European call option with an exercise price of $21. The risk free rate is 12% per year. Three months from now the option is worth $1 (in good state) or $0 (in bad state). If we create a portfolio that is long .25 shares of stock and short 1 call we will show that in both Good and Bad states this portfolio yields $4.50.

State	Portfolio Value
Good	.25($22) –(1)($1) = $4.50.
Bad	.25($18) –(1)($0) = $4.50.

Note that in the Good state the option is worth $1 because we can exercise the option and buy the stock for $20 and immediately sell the stock for $21. In the Bad state the option is worthless because there is no benefit to be gained by buying the stock for $20 when the current price is $18!

Since this portfolio yields $4.50 for certain three months from now its value today must equal the NPV (discounted at the risk-free rate) of $4.50 received three months from now. This is just

$$4.5e^{-.25(.12)} = \$4.37.$$

This implies that

$$.25(today's\ stock\ price) - (today's\ option\ price) = \$4.37,$$

or

$$5 - (today's\ option\ price) = \$4.37,$$

or

$$(today's\ option\ price) = \$0.63.$$

This pricing approach is called *arbitrage pricing*. The argument works independent of a person's risk preferences. Therefore we may use the following approach to price derivatives:

1. In a world where everyone is risk neutral arbitrage pricing is valid.

2. In a risk neutral world all assets must grow on average at risk free rate.

3. In a risk neutral world any asset (including an option) is worth the expected value of its discounted cash flows.

4. Set up a risk neutral world in which all stocks grow at risk free rate and use @RISK (or binomial tree; see Chapters 56-58 of Winston (1998)) to determine expected discounted cash flows from option.

5. Since the arbitrage pricing method gives the correct price in all worlds *it yields the correct price in a risk neutral world.* Therefore *if we use the above method to find a derivative's price in a risk neutral world, we have found the right price for our complicated non-risk neutral world!*

It is important to note that actual growth rate of a stock is irrelevant to pricing a derivative. Information about a stock's future growth rate is imbedded in today's stock price.

Example of Risk Neutral Approach

Let's find the call option value of $0.63 using the risk neutral approach. Let p be probability (in the risk neutral world) that in 3 months stock price is $22. Then 1 – p is probability that stock price 3 months from now is $18. If stock grows on average at risk free rate we must have

$$p(\$22) + (1-p)(\$18) = 20 * e^{(.25)(.12)} = \$20.61,$$

or

$$4p = 2.61$$

or

$$p = .65.$$

Now value option as expected discounted value of its cash flows:

$$e^{-.25(.12)}(.65(\$1) + .35(\$0)) = \$0.63.$$

For further discussion of the risk neutral approach we refer the reader to Hull (1997).

References:

Hull, J. *Options Futures and Derivative Securities*, Prentice-Hall, 1997.
Winston, W. L. , *Financial Modeling Using Simulation and Optimization*, Palisade Corporation, 1998.

Chapter 26: The Lognormal Model of Stock Prices

The Lognormal model for asset value (or stock price) assumes that in a small time Δt the stock price changes by an amount that is normally distributed with

$$Mean = \mu S \Delta t$$

$$Standard\ Deviation = \sigma S \sqrt{\Delta t}$$

Here S = current stock price.

The variable μ may be thought of as the instantaneous rate of return on the stock. By the way, this model leads to really "jumpy" changes in stock prices (like real life). This is because during a small period of time the standard deviation of the stock's movement will greatly exceed the mean of a stock's movement. This follows because for small Δt, $\sqrt{\Delta t}$ will be much larger than Δt.

In a small time Δt the natural logarithm (Ln (S)) of the current stock price will change (by Ito's Lemma, see Hull (1997)) by an amount that is normally distributed with

$$Mean = (\mu - .5\sigma^2)\Delta t$$

$$Standard\ Deviation = \sigma \sqrt{\Delta t}$$

Let S_t = stock price at time t. In Chapter 11 of Hull (1997) it is shown that at time t Ln S_t is normally distributed with

$$Mean = Ln\ S_0 + (\mu - .5\sigma^2)\ t$$

$$Standard\ Deviation = \sigma \sqrt{t}$$

We refer to $(\mu - .5\sigma^2)$ as the ***continuously compounded rate of return*** on the stock. Note the continuously compounded rate of return on S is less than instantaneous return. Since Ln S_t follows a normal random variable we say that S_t is a ***Lognormal random variable.***

To simulate S_t we get Ln (S_t) by entering in @RISK the formula

$$= LN(S_0) + (\mu - .5\sigma^2)t + \sigma\sqrt{t}\,RiskNormal(0,1)$$

Therefore to get S_t we must take the antilog of this equation and get

$$S_t = S_0 e^{(\mu - .5\sigma^2)t + \sigma\sqrt{t}\,RiskNormal(0,1)} \tag{26.1}$$

Risk Neutral Valuation

To apply the risk neutral valuation approach of Chapter 25 we assume the asset grows at instantaneous rate r. ***Then the value of a derivative is simply the expected discounted (at risk free rate) value of cash flows***. We will often apply this approach. We can estimate volatility by implied volatility (see Chapter 27) or historical volatility (see below).

Historical Estimation of Mean and Volatility of Stock Return

If we average values of

$$Ln \frac{S_t}{S_{t-1}}$$

we obtain an estimate of $(\mu - .5\sigma^2)$.

If we take the standard deviation of

$$Ln \frac{S_t}{S_{t-1}}$$

we obtain an estimate of σ.

Using monthly returns of Dell Computer for 1988-1996 we may estimate μ and σ. See the Figure 26.1 and the file Dell.xls.

Figure 26.1

	A	B	C	D	E	F
1		estimate of	monthly			
2		mu-.5*sigma^2	0.034572			
3		sigma	0.160929			
4	DATE	Dell	Ln(1+Dell)			
5	6/30/88				monthly estimate	
6	7/29/88	0.106667	0.101353		sigma	0.160929
7	8/31/88	-0.228916	-0.25996		mu	0.047521
8	9/30/88	0.28125	0.247836		annual estimate	
9	10/31/88	0.158537	0.147158		sigma	0.557473
10	11/30/88	-0.0842105	-0.08797		mu	0.570254
11	12/30/88	-0.0804598	-0.08388			
12	1/31/89	-0.05	-0.05129			
13	2/28/89	-0.171053	-0.1876			
14	3/31/89	-0.0952381	-0.10008			
15	4/28/89	0.105263	0.100083			
16	5/31/89	0.0793651	0.076373			
17	6/30/89	-0.0735294	-0.07637			
18	7/31/89	-0.142857	-0.15415			
19	8/31/89	0.037037	0.036368			
20	9/29/89	0.0178571	0.0177			
21	10/31/89	-0.157895	-0.17185			
22	11/30/89	-0.0416667	-0.04256			
23	12/29/89	-0.0434783	-0.04445			
24	1/31/90	-0.159091	-0.17327			
25	2/28/90	0.351351	0.301105			
26	3/30/90	0.22	0.198851			
27	4/30/90	0.114754	0.108634			
99	4/30/96	0.369403	0.314375			
100	5/31/96	0.207084	0.188208			
101	6/28/96	-0.0812641	-0.08476			
102	7/31/96	0.0909091	0.087011			
103	8/30/96	0.209459	0.190173			
104	9/30/96	0.158287	0.146942			
105	10/31/96	0.0466238	0.04557			
106	11/29/96	0.248848	0.222222			
107	12/31/96	0.0455105	0.044505			

We begin by estimating σ and μ for a monthly lognormal process. Then our estimate of σ for an annual lognormal process is just $\sqrt{12}$ (monthly estimate of σ) and our estimate of μ for an annual lognormal process is just 12*(monthly estimate of μ).

Step by Step   **Step 1: Note that for any month** $\frac{S_{t+1}}{S_t} = \left(1 + (Month\ Return)_t\right)$. Therefore in

C6:C107 we compute for each month $Ln\frac{S_{t+1}}{S_t}$ by copying from C6 to C7:C107 the

formula

=LN(1+B6).

Step 2: In C2 we estimate μ -.5σ^2 with the formula

=AVERAGE(C6:C107).

Step 3: In C3 we estimate σ with the formula

=STDEV(C6:C107).

Step 4: In cell F7 we find our estimate of μ for a monthly lognormal process with the formula

=C2+0.5*F6^2.

Thus for the monthly lognormal we estimate for Dell Computer that μ = .0475 and σ = .161.

Step 5: In cells F9 and F10 we find our annualized estimates of μ and σ with the formulas

=12*F7 *(for μ)*

=SQRT(12)*F6. *(for σ)*.

Our annualized estimates are μ = 57.0% and σ = 55.7%.

Finding Mean and Variance of a Lognormal Random Variable

It is important to point out that μ is not actually the mean of a Lognormal random variable and σ is not really the standard deviation. Assume a stock follows a Lognormal random variable with parameters μ and σ. Let S = current price of stock (which is known) and S_t = Price of stock at time t (unknown). Then (see page 310 of Luenberger (1997)) the mean and variance of S_t are as follows:

$$Mean\ of\ S_t = Se^{\mu t}$$

$$Variance\ of\ S_t = S^2 e^{2\mu t}(e^{\sigma^2 t} - 1)$$

The file Lognormal.xls contains a template to determine the mean and variance of a stock price at any future time. See Figure 26.2.

Figure 26.2

	A	B	C	D
2				
3	S=current price	20		
4	t=time	1		
5	mu	0.2		
6	sigma	0.4		
7	alpha	0.95		
8				
9	Mean for ln S(T)	3.115732	Mean S(T)	24.42806
10	Sigma for ln S(T)	0.4	var S(T)	103.5391
11			sigma S(T)	10.17542
12	CI			
13	Lower(for ln S(T))	2.331748		
14	Upper (for ln S(T))	3.899717		
15	Lower for S(T)	10.29592		
16	Upper for S(T)	49.38846		

For example, consider a Stock currently selling for $20 following a lognormal random variable with μ = .20 and σ = .40. The mean stock price one year from now is $24.43 with a standard deviation of $10.18.

Confidence Intervals for a Lognormal Random Variable

The file Lognormal.xls computes a confidence interval for a future stock price. If you want a 95% Confidence interval enter .95 for alpha, etc. From Figure 26.2 we find that for a stock currently selling for $20 with μ = .20 and σ = .40, we are 95% sure that the price of the stock one year from now will be between $10.30 and $49.39.

Remark

There is a lot of evidence that changes in stock prices have "fatter tails" than a Lognormal random variable. Despite this evidence, the lognormal random variable is still widely used to model changes in stock prices. For foreign exchange rates, however, the recent Asian financial crisis demonstrated that sudden jumps in exchange rates are fairly common. Sudden jumps in exchange rates or stock prices can be modeled with a **jump diffusion** process which combines a "jump process" with a Lognormal process. It is usually assumed that the number of jumps per unit time follows a Poisson random variable and the size of each jump (as a percentage of the current price) follows a normal distribution. See Chapter 19 of Hull (1997) for a brief discussion of the jump diffusion process.

Reference

Hull, J. Options Futures and Derivative Securities, Prentice-Hall, 1997.
Winston, W., *Financial Models Using Simulation and Optimization*, Palisade, 1998.

Chapter 27: Optimal Hedging of Dell Computer Investment

When we own a stock such as Dell Computer, there is always a risk that the stock will go down. If we buy puts on the stock, then the puts increase in value when the stock price drops below the put's exercise price. Therefore purchasing puts can lessen the risk involved in owning a stock. In this chapter we show how to use RISKOptimizer to choose the number of puts to purchase for hedging investment risk. We begin by showing how the risk neutral approach described in Chapter 25 can be combined with Monte Carlo simulation to price options. Then we show how to use RISKOptimizer to obtain an optimal hedging policy.

Estimating Volatility

Even though European puts and calls can easily be priced by the Black-Scholes (BS) formula, it is instructive to use Monte Carlo simulation to price European options. The file option.xls contains a template that gives the BS price for a European put or call.

Of course, the key input into pricing an option is the stock's *volatility.* This is just the value of σ in the lognormal representation of the stock's price. In Chapter 26 we showed how historical data could be used to estimate σ. *Implied volatility* is a more commonly used method for estimating a stock's volatility. Given the price of an option, the stock's implied volatility is the value of σ which makes the BS price for the option match the actual price. In a sense the volatility estimate is "implied" by the actual option price. We now show how to use Goal Seek to find an implied volatility. We note that the risk free rate input to the BS formula should be the continuously compounded rate, or *Ln(1+ current 90 day T-Bill Rate).*

Example 27.1

On June 30, 1998 Dell Computer sold for $94. A European put with an exercise price of $80 expiring on November 22, 1998 was selling for $5.25. The current 90 day T-Bill rate is 5.5%. What is the implied volatility of Dell Computer?

Solution

Our work is in the file option.xls. See Figure 27.1.

Figure 27.1

	A	B	C	D	E	F
1	**Black-Schole's Option Pricing Problem**					
2	**Using the Option Price to Find the Implied Volatility**					
3						
4	Input data					
5	Stock price	$94			today	6/30/98
6	Exercise price	$80			expire	11/22/98
7	Duration	0.39726				
8	Interest rate	5.35%				
9						
10	Implied volatility (stdev)	53.27%				
11						
12	Call price	Actual		Predicted		
13			=	$21.06		
14	Put price	$5.25		$5.25		
15						
16						
17	Other quantities for option price					
18	d1	0.715534		N(d1)	0.76286	
19	d2	0.37981		N(d2)	0.647957	

Step by Step

Step 1: Enter the duration of the option (145/365) years in B7, the current stock and exercise prices in B5 and B6, and in B8 the risk free rate Ln(1+.055).

Step 2: Now use Goal Seek (see below) to change the volatility until the predicted BS price for a put matches *actual* price.

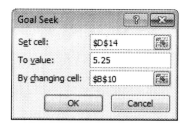

We change volatility (B10) until predicted put price (D14) equals $5.25 (actual put price). From Figure 27.1 we obtain a 53.27% annual volatility. Interestingly enough, in Chapter 26 historical data indicated 55.7% volatility.

Remark

If you want Excel to figure out the duration of the option enter the current date and expiration dates with the DATEVALUE function and subtract them. To do this we entered in cell G5 the formula

$$=DATEVALUE("6/30/98")$$

and in cell G6 the formula

$$=DATEVALUE("11/22/98").$$

See Figure 27.2. Note that the DATEVALUE function yields the number of days the date is after January 1, 1900.

Figure 27.2

	E	F	G
4			
5	today	6/30/98	35976
6	expire	11/22/98	36121
7			145.00

Using Simulation to Price the Put

Now we will use Monte Carlo Simulation to price the put. We begin by entering relevant parameters in cells B2:B4 of sheet Dell Sim in file Option.xls. Recall from Chapter 25 that a fair price for the put is the *expected discounted value of the put's cash flows in a risk neutral world.* In a risk neutral world, the stock will grow at the risk free rate. Therefore we will use (26.1) with μ = risk free rate to price the put. We have used the following range names:

- r_ = the risk free rate
- p = The current stock price
- v = volatility
- d = duration
- x = exercise price

Figure 27.3

	A	B	C	D	E
1	Pricing Put by Simulation				
2	Current stock price	$ 94.00		95% CI	
3	Risk free rate	0.053541		Lower Limit	5.090718
4	Duration	0.39726		Upper Limit	5.469088
5	volatility	53.265%			
6	Exercise price	$ 80.00			
7	Stock price at expiration	91.93506			Name
8	Put cash flows at expiration	0			Description
9	Discounted value of put cash flows	0			Cell

We proceed as follows:

Step by Step

Step 1: In cell B7 we use (26.1) to generate Dell's price at the expiration date with the formula

$=p*EXP((r\_-0.5*v^2)*d+RiskNormal(0,1)*v*SQRT(d))$.

Step 2: In cell B8 we compute the cash flows from the put. Recall a put pays nothing if Dell's price on the expiration date exceeds $80; otherwise the put pays $80 - (Dell price at expiration).

$=IF(B7>x,0,x-B7)$.

Step 3: In cell B9 we compute the expected discounted value of the put's cash flows with the formula

$=EXP(-r\_*d)*B8$.

Step 4: We select B9 as our output cell and ran 10,000 iterations. From Figure 27.4

Figure 27.4

	D	E
2	95% CI	
3	Lower Limit	5.090718
4	Upper Limit	5.469088

	E	F
9	Cell	B9
10	Minimum =	0
11	Maximum	57.99311
12	Mean =	5.279903
13	Std Deviati	9.459261
14	Variance =	89.47761
15	Skewness	1.900912
16	Kurtosis =	5.931631
17	Errors Calc	0
18	Mode =	0
19	5% Perc =	0
20	10% Perc	0
21	15% Perc	0
22	20% Perc	0
23	25% Perc	0
24	30% Perc	0
25	35% Perc	0
26	40% Perc	0
27	45% Perc	0
28	50% Perc	0
29	55% Perc	0
30	60% Perc	0
31	65% Perc	0.246574
32	70% Perc	3.815132
33	75% Perc	7.46743
34	80% Perc	11.33537
35	85% Perc	15.56934
36	90% Perc	20.52942
37	95% Perc	27.15265

Our best estimate of the put price is $5.28. We are 95% sure that the put price is between $5.09 and $5.47 (see cells E3 and E4). After 10,000 iterations why is our confidence interval so wide? The reason is that this put only pays off on very *extreme results* (Dell's price dropping a lot). It takes many iterations to accurately represent extreme values of a Lognormal random variable.

Remark

If the stock pays dividends at a rate q% per year, then in a risk neutral world the stock price must grow at a rate r - q. Therefore, for stocks that pay dividends at a rate of q% per year, we should price their options by using (26.1) with r - q replacing r.

Value at Risk

Anybody who owns a portfolio of investments knows there is a great deal of uncertainty about the future worth of the portfolio. Recently the concept of *value at risk (VAR)* has been used to help describe a portfolio's uncertainty. Simply stated, value at risk of a portfolio at a future point in time is usually considered to be the fifth percentile of the loss in the portfolio's value at that point in time. In short, there is considered to be only one chance in 20 that the portfolio's loss will exceed the VAR. To illustrate the idea suppose a portfolio today is worth $100. We simulate the portfolio's value one year from now and find there is a 5% chance that the portfolio's value will be $80 or less. Then the portfolio's VAR is $20 or 20%. The following example shows how RISKOptimizer can be used to control VAR. The example also demonstrates how buying puts can greatly reduce the risk, or *hedge*, a long position in a stock.

Example 27.2   Let's suppose we own one share of Dell Computer on June 30, 1998. The current price is $94. From historical data (see Figure 26.1) we have estimated that the growth of the price of Dell stock can be modeled as a Lognormal random variable with μ = 57% and σ = 55.7%. To hedge the risk involved in owning Dell we are considering buying (for $5.25) some European puts on Dell with exercise price $80 and expiration date November 22, 1998. How many puts on Dell should we buy to maximize our expected return, while maintaining a VAR of at most -20% or better?

Solution   The key idea is to realize that in valuing the put we let Dell price grow at the risk-free rate, but when doing a VAR calculation we should let Dell price grow at the rate at which we expect it to grow. Our work is in file vardell.xls. See Figure 27.5.

Figure 27.5

	A	B	C	D	E
2	Dell	Range Name			
3	Current price	S	$ 94.00		
4	Put exercise price	x	$ 80.00		
5	put duration	d	0.39726		
6	risk free rate	r_	0.053541		
7	actual growth rate	g	0.57		
8	volatility	v	0.557		
9	put price	p	$ 5.25		
10	puts bought		2.118606307		
11	Dell price at expiration		110.8422852		
12	put value at expiration		0		
13	%age Gain with put		5.4%	Mean = .2195	
14	Percentile		-0.199999372 ◄———		
15					

We have created range names as indicated in Figure 27.5.

Step 1: In cell B11 we generate Dell's price on November 22, 1998 with the formula

$$=S*EXP((g-0.5*v^\wedge 2)*d+RiskNormal(0,1)*v*SQRT(d)).$$

Step 2: In cell B12 we compute the payments from the put at expiration with the formula

$$=IF(B11>x,0,x-B11).$$

Step 3: In cell B10 we enter a trial value for the number of puts purchased.

Step 4: The percentage gain on our portfolio is calculated using this formula:

$$\frac{Ending\ Dell\ Price + (B10)*Cash\ Flows\ from\ Put - Beginning\ Dell\ Price - B10*Put\ Price}{Beginning\ Dell\ Price + B10*Put\ Price}$$

In cell B13 we compute the percentage gain on our portfolio

$$=((B10*B12+B11)-(S+B10*p))/(S+B10*p).$$

Step 5: In cell B14 we compute the VAR (or 5th percentile) of our return with the formula

$$=RiskPercentile(B13,0.05).$$

For each number of puts purchased tried by RISKOptimizer this formula computes the 5th percentile of the portfolio's return.

Step 6: We are now ready to use RISKOptimizer to find the portfolio that maximizes our mean return and has a VAR of -20% or better. Our Model window follows:

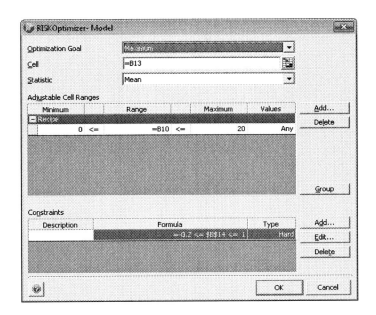

We want to maximize our portfolio's mean return (cell B13) by adjusting the number of puts purchased (cell B10). We restrict number of puts purchased to between 0 and 20. The second constraint ensures that our VAR is at least -20%. RISKOptimizer recommends buying 2.12 puts. A mean return of around 22% is obtained while our VAR is almost exactly -20%.

Maximizing the Sharpe Ratio

A common goal in investments is to choose a portfolio that maximizes the *Sharpe Ratio*. The Sharpe Ratio is defined to equal $\dfrac{\mu - r}{\sigma}$, where

> μ = Portfolio mean
> σ = Portfolio standard deviation
> r = risk-free rate

Intuitively, the Sharpe ratio maximizes the excess (over risk-free rate) mean return per unit of portfolio risk. RISKOptimizer can easily find a portfolio maximizing the Sharpe Ratio. See Figure 27.6 and file Dell2.xls.

Figure 27.6

	A	B	C	D
2	Dell	Range Name		
3	Current price	S	$ 94.00	
4	Put exercise price	x	$ 80.00	
5	put duration	d	0.39726	
6	risk free rate	r_	0.053541	
7	actual growth rate	g	0.57	
8	volatility	v	0.557	
9	put price	p	$ 5.25	
10	puts bought	2.51430768		
11	Dell price at expiration	110.8422852		
12	put value at expiration	0		
13	%age Gain with put	3.4%		
14	Percentile	-0.212885743		
15	Mean	0.235137923		
16	Standard deviation	0.394736995		
17	Sharpe Ratio	0.46004595		
18				
19				
20				
21				46

Step by Step

Our changes from the previous spreadsheet follow:

Step 1: In B15 have RISKOptimizer track the mean portfolio return with the formula

> *=RiskMean(B13).*

Step 2: In B16 have RISKOptimizer track the standard deviation of the portfolio return with the formula

> *=RiskStdDev(B13).*

Step 3: In B17 we compute the Sharpe Ratio with the formula

$=(B15-r\_)/B16.$

Step 4: We now use RISKOptimizer to determine the number of puts to purchase to maximize the Sharpe Ratio.

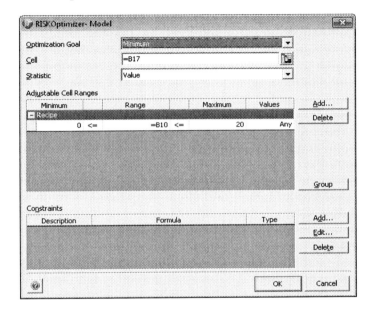

We choose to maximize the Sharpe ratio (cell B17) by adjusting the number of puts purchased (B10). We constrain the number of puts purchased to be between 0 and 20. The maximum Sharpe ratio of .46 is obtained by purchasing 2.51 puts.

Chapter 28: Foreign Exchange Options and Hedging Foreign Exchange Risk

In the file fx.xls you have a template that uses the BS model to price European foreign exchange puts and calls. Note that an additional input is the interest rate in the foreign country. Letting r = US interest rate and q = Foreign interest rate we can also price a foreign exchange option (even an exotic) via simulation *by assuming the exchange rate ($s per unit of foreign currency) grows at a rate r – q.*

Example 28.1   On July 31, 1997 exchange rate was $.5445/ mark. Price of a European put option expiring on September 21, 1997 with exercise price $.53/mark was 0.23 cents. US interest rate was 5.1% and German interest rate was 2.5%.

     a.   What is implied volatility?

     b.   We have 500,000 marks coming on September 21 1997. How many puts should we buy to minimize the standard deviation of the dollar amount of our portfolio?

Solution -
Part a   Putting all our known inputs into the option template we may find the implied volatility of the $/mark rate using goal seek.

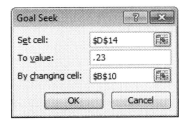

Thus we try to adjust the volatility (B10) so that cell D14 becomes .23. We find

The implied volatility is 9.9%.

Figure 28.1

	A	B	C	D	E	F
1	**Currency**					
2	**Option Template**					
3				July 31, 1997 data		
4	Input data			Today's September put price		
5	Currency value in $s	$0.5445		.23 cents		
6	Exercise price	$0.5300				
7	Duration	0.142466				
8	Interest rate	0.051				
9	Foreign interest rate	0.026				
10	Implied volatility	0.098567				
11				cents		
12				Predicted		
13		Call Price		1.86247		
14		Put Price		0.230096		
15	Other quantities for option price					
16	d1	0.839829		N(d1)	0.799498	
17	d2	0.802625		N(d2)	0.788904	
18				N(-d1)	0.200502	
19				N(-d2)	0.211096	
20						
21						

Solution - Part b

We now simulate our dollar cash flows on September 21 corresponding to receiving 500,000 marks and buying, say, 8 puts on 62,500 marks (see Figure 28.2).

Figure 28.2

	A	B	C	D	E	F
1		**500,000 dm coming on september 21**				
2						
3		Payments	500000			
4		Put price today	0.23	cents!!		
5		r	0.051			
6		implied vol	0.0985			
7		r foreign	0.026		Discounted cash flow from put	
8		duration	0.142466		0	
9		$/dm today	0.5445			
10		$/dm on Sept 21	0.546065			
11		Put strike price	0.53			
12		**Puts bought**	17	62,500 dm/put		
13		$ value in September				
14		Payments	273032.6			
15		Put option received	0			
16		Cost	2461.57			
17		Total with hedge	270571.1			
18		Std dev	7707.38			
19						
20						
21				StdDev = 7707.3797		
22						

Step 1: We enter all input parameters in C3:C9. Note duration =52/365=.14. Also in cell C12 we enter a trial number of puts purchased.

Step 2: Assuming $/mark grows at rate (.051-.026) per year we can generate in cell C10 the September 21 $/mark price with the formula

=C9*EXP((C5-C7-0.5*C6^2)*C8+C6*RiskNormal(0,1)*SQRT(C8)).

Step 3: In C14 we convert our 500,000 marks to dollars with the formula

=C3*C10.

Step 4: In C15 we compute the payment (in dollars) received on September 21 from our put options with the formula

=C12*62500*MAX(C11-C10,0).

Step 5: In C16 we compute the cost of the put options in September 21 dollars (remembering to compute its future value!) with the formula

=EXP(C8*C5)*C4*C12*62500/100.

Note that price of put is in cents so we divide by 100 to go back to dollars!

Step 6: In C17 we compute our total $'s received with the formula

= C14+C15-C16.

Step 7: We are now ready to use RISKOptimizer to determine the number of puts that should be purchased in order to minimize the standard deviation of the dollar value of our assets.

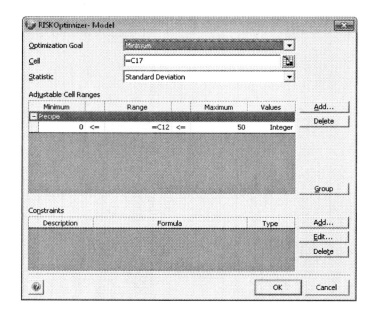

We choose to minimize the standard deviation of our dollar value (cell C17) by changing the number of puts (cell C12) purchased. We constrain the number of puts to be an integer between 0 and 50. RISKOptimizer finds that the standard deviation of our assets can be reduced to $7707 by purchasing 17 puts. Using @RISK we found that if we bought no puts, the standard deviation of the dollar value of our Dm receipts was $10,200. Thus our hedging has reduced the standard deviation by 24%.

Hedging a Minor Currency with a Related Currency

Options on minor currencies are often unavailable or illiquid. How can we lessen the risk associated with cash receipts in minor currencies? Probably the easiest way is to take a short position in a related major currency. The following example, based on Luenberger (1997) shows how this is done.

Example 28.2   Two months from now we will receive 1,000,000 Danish Kroner. Usually the Kroner and the mark move together. Therefore we can reduce the exchange rate risk associated with our Kroner receipts by shorting German Marks. We assume that the dollar value of the Kroner and mark can be modeled as Lognormal random variables. We are given the following information:

- Current value of Kroner: $.164.
- Current value of Mark: $.625
- Monthly sigma for dollar value of Kroner = 0.025.
- Monthly sigma for dollar value of Mark =0.03.
- Correlation between currency movements = 0.80.

The mean monthly change in each currency's monthly value is irrelevant and may be assumed to equal 0. How many Marks should be shorted to minimize the standard deviation of our dollar position?

Solution   Our work is in file kroner.xls and Figure 28.3.

Step by Step   **Step 1: In cell B11 enter a trial number of Marks shorted.**

Step 2: In B14 and B15 generate the exchange rate for Kroner and Marks. We use the =RiskCorrmat function and equation (26.1). In B14 we generate the exchange rate for Kroner two months hence with the formula

    =RiskCorrmat(F12:G13,1)+B3*EXP((C6-0.5*B6^2)*$B$10+B6* RiskNormal(0,1)*SQRT($B$10)).

In B15 we generate the exchange rate for Marks two months hence with the formula

    =RiskCorrmat(F12:G13,2)+B4*EXP((C7-0.5*B7^2)*B10+B7* RiskNormal(0,1)*SQRT(B10)).

The *RiskCorrmat(F12:G13,1)* and *RiskCorrmat(F12:G13,2)* functions ensure that $/Kroner and will be correlated with a correlation of .8. The "+" ensures that the distribution of each exchange rate will be computed in accordance with what is after the "+" sign, which is the Lognormal random variable.

Figure 28.3

	A	B	C	D	E	F	G
1	**Hedging Kroner**						
2	**Current values**						
3	$/kroner	0.164					
4	$/dm	0.625					
5	**Monthly par**	sigma	mu				
6	$/kroner	0.025	0				
7	$/mark	0.03	0				
8							
9	Correlation	0.8					
10	Duration	2					
11	dm shorted	192869				Correlation matrix	
12	kroner received	1000000				1	0.8
13	**Two month rates**					0.8	1
14	$/kroner	0.163897532					
15	$/mark	0.624437753				Original sigma 5805	
16							
17	Final dollar value						
18	kroner	163897.532					
19	profit on marks	108.4400072					
20	total	164005.972					
21							
22							
23				StdDev = 3525.1966			
24							

Step 3: In B18 we compute the $ value of our Kroner with the formula

=B14*B12.

Step 4: In B19 we compute the profit earned from our short position in Marks. Note that this profit equals

=(B4-B15)*B11.

Since we are shorting Marks, we *gain* money if $/Marks decreases. Since a decrease in $/Mark tends to occur (because of the .8 correlation) when $/Kroner also decreases, we can see that we have created a hedge. Similarly, if $/Mark increase, we lose money on our short position, but we probably make money on our Kroner position. Thus no matter what happens, we have used our short position in Marks to hedge our risk.

Step 5: Our total final $ position is computed in B20 by adding our Mark profit and final value of Kroner position.

=B18+B19.

Step 6: We are now ready to use RISKOptimizer to find the number of Marks to short that minimizes the standard deviation of our final position.

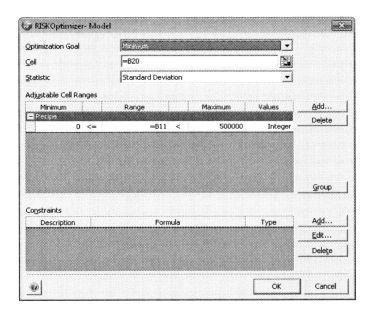

We minimize the standard deviation of our final $ position (cell B20) by adjusting the number of Marks shorted (B11). We constrain the number of Marks shorted to be an integer between 0 and 500,000. RISKOptimizer recommends shorting 192,869 Marks. This yields a standard deviation of $3525 in our final dollar position. If we had shorted no Marks, an @RISK simulation shows that the standard deviation of our dollar position would have been $5805. Thus shorting Marks reduced our risk by around 40%.

Reference
Luenberger, D., *Investment Science,* Oxford Press, 1997.

Chapter 29: Hedging with Futures

Many corporations face the risk that their profit will greatly change when commodity prices or currency rates change. For example, a glass making company uses natural gas to heat their furnaces. They face the risk that the price of gas will increase, thereby increasing their costs. A drug company selling drugs in Germany faces the risk that a decline in the value of the mark will reduce the value of their German accounts receivable. *Futures and forwards* can be used to hedge commodity and exchange risk.

In this Chapter we give a brief introduction to futures. Then we show how to use RISKOptimizer to determine optimal hedging policies.

Suppose you have just bought an ounce of gold for $300. The current price of a commodity such as gold is called the *spot price* of the commodity. If the price of gold increases, you make money because your gold is worth more. If the price of gold decreases, however, you will lose money. To reduce or *hedge* this risk you might sell or *short* a gold future. Suppose today is January 1, 2000 and you have sold or shorted a one-year gold future. This means that on January 1, 2001 you have a guarantee that you will be paid an amount (the current one-year futures price) and in return you must deliver on that date one ounce of gold. This obligation may be traded at any time on a futures exchange for the current futures price of a January 1, 2001 future. As time progresses, if the market deems gold more valuable the value of the gold you own goes up, but you lose money on your futures contract because you will have to deliver a more valuable commodity. If as time progresses the market deems gold less valuable you lose money on your gold, but the value of your futures contract increases because you will have to deliver a less valuable commodity. This discussion shows that by selling or shorting a gold future we can reduce the risk involved in holding gold.

Pricing of Futures Contracts

Simple formulas exist (see Chapter 3 of Hull (1997)) for the price of forward contracts. Forward contracts cannot be traded month to month. We will assume the formulas for forward prices apply to futures prices. Let S = current spot price of a commodity and r = risk free rate. Then ignoring storage costs and convenience yields the price of a futures contract expiring at time T is given by

$$F = Se^{rT}$$

(29.1).

The natural question is, of course, how many futures do you need to buy to adequately hedge your risk? In this chapter we show how to use RISKOptimizer to determine optimal hedging policies. Our goal will be to choose a hedging policy that minimizes the standard deviation of our total costs.

An Overview of Hedging

Suppose I need to purchase heating oil in November 2000. Also suppose that on June 8 of 2000 I purchase (or *go long*) a December 2000 future for a price of $1 per barrel. This gives me the right to receive a barrel of heating oil for $1 on December 8, 2000. Suppose the price of heating oil increases, and I close out my futures contract on November 1, 2000 and buy heating oil. What happens? The cost of heating oil increases (this is bad for me) but the value of the future contract increases (this is good for me) because I have the right to receive a more valuable commodity. If the price of heating oil drops between June and December what happens? The drop in the cost of heating oil reduces my cost of purchasing oil (this is good) but the value of the future drops (this is bad) because I have the right to receive a less valuable commodity. In short, going long the future has created a hedge that makes the change in the price of heating oil between June and December largely irrelevant.

Suppose I own an ounce of gold on June 8, 2000. If I sell or short one December 8, 2000 gold future at $400 what can happen? Shorting the future means I must deliver an ounce of gold (and receive $400) on December 8, 2000. If the price of gold increases, the value of my gold increases (this is good) but the value of my future drops (this is bad) because I must deliver a more valuable commodity. If the price of gold drops then the value of my gold drops (this is bad), but the value of the shorted future increases (this is good) because I must deliver a less valuable commodity. Thus we see that shorting the future has created a hedge that makes the change in the price of gold largely irrelevant.

We now turn to a specific example of how to determine how many futures to purchase when hedging. We will deal with the previously discussed oil situation. Recall from (29.1) that given the current risk free rate r and the current spot price S a futures contract of duration T should sell for Se^{rT}. In reality, however, future prices will vary about this "expected price". Let's suppose that for oil futures, actual future prices average out to the prediction of (29.1) with a standard deviation of 5%. The other source of uncertainty is, of course, the spot price path of oil in later months. We will assume that future oil prices will be governed by a Lognormal random variable, so future spot prices may be modeled with (26.1).

Example 29.1 It is June 8, 2000. Glassco needs to purchase 500,000 gallons of heating oil on November 8, 2000. The current spot price of oil is $0.42 per gallon. Oil prices are assumed to follow a Lognormal random variable with $\mu = .08$ and $\sigma = .30$. The risk free rate is 6%. We are hedging the price risk inherent in our future oil purchase by buying oil futures that expire on December 8, 2000. How many futures should we buy? We assume the mean future price at any time is governed by (29.1) and the actual future price will have a standard deviation equal to 5% of its mean. We assume that on June 8, 2000 the December 8, 2000 oil future is selling for $0.43769. We also ignore movements in the interest rate.

Solution Our work is in the file future.xls. See Figure 29.1

Step by Step **Step 1: In B6:B11 we enter relevant parameters.**

Step 2: In B12 we enter the price of the December future on June 8 ($0.43769).

Step 3: In B13 we enter number of gallons of heating oil that must be purchased.

Step 4: In B14 we enter a trial number of gallons of heating oil futures to purchase.

Step 5: In B15 we use (26.1) to generate the November 8 spot oil price.

=B6*EXP((B9-0.5*B8^2)*(5/12)+RiskNormal(0,1)*SQRT(5/12)*B8).

Step 6: In B16 we use (29.1) to compute the expected price of the December future on November 8

=EXP((1/12)*B7)*B15.

Step 7 In B17 we build in the 5% standard deviation of the actual future price from the expected future price and compute the actual price of the December future on November 8.

=RiskNormal(B16,B16*B10).

Step 8: In B19 we compute the cost of buying oil at the November 8 spot price with the formula

=B15*B13.

Step 9: In B20 we compute the revenue earned from selling our futures on November 8 with the formula

=B17*B14.

Figure 29.1

	A	B	C	D	E
1	**Hedging**				
2	**Petroleum**		Future expires December 8		
3	**Risk**				
4					
5					
6	June 8 oil price per gallon	0.42			
7	r	0.06			
8	volatility	0.3			
9	oil drift	0.08			
10	sigma of percentage variation of future from mean	0.05			
11	future duration	0.5			Iterations= 400
12	December futures price on June 8	0.43769			
13	gallons bought	500000			
14	# long	478150			
15	November 8 spot oil price	0.426169879			
16	Mean of November 8 price of December future	0.428306065			
17	Actual November 8 futures price	0.428306065			
18	**Bottom line**				
19	Cost of buying oil	$ 213,084.94			
20	Revenue from futures	$ 204,794.54			
21	Cost of buying futures on June 8	$ 209,281.47			
22	Total cost	$ 217,571.87			
23					
24					
25				StdDev = 10784.4059	
26					

Step 10: In B21 we compute the cost of buying our futures on June 8 with the formula

$=B12*B14.$

Step 11: In B22 we compute our total cost (oil purchase cost) + (futures purchase cost) - (futures sales revenue) with the formula

$=B19+B21-B20.$

Step 12: We now use RISKOptimizer to determine how many gallons of heating oil futures to purchase.

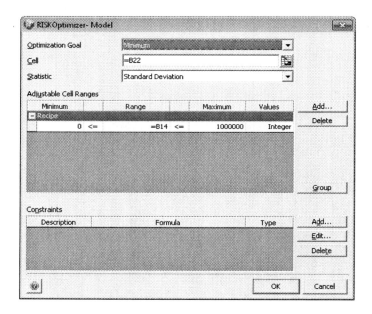

We choose to minimize the standard deviation of our total cost (cell B22) by adjusting the number of heating oil futures (B14) purchased. RISKOptimizer reduces the standard deviation of our cost to $10,784 by purchasing 478,150 gallons of oil futures.

Hedging Commodity Risk when Production is Correlated with Price

Suppose Farmer Jones produces wheat. Most wheat in US is produced in the Midwest, so if Farmer Jones produces a lot of wheat the odds are most of the Midwest wheat farmers had a good year. This will, unfortunately, reduce the price of wheat for Farmer Jones. Can Farmer Jones use RISKOptimizer to optimally hedge his price and production risk? Our example is based on Luenberger (1997). Our work is in file corn.xls. See Figure 29.2.

Example 29.2 Farmer Jones believes that the amount of wheat produced on his one-acre farm follows a normal random variable (due to weather uncertainty) with mean 3000 bushels and standard deviation 1000 bushels. To simplify matters assume the US has a total of 100 wheat farmers, and each Farmer's production will equal Farmer Jones' production. The price per bushel of wheat today is given by

10-(Total Production)/100,000.

Thus, for example, if 500,000 bushels are produced the price of wheat will equal $5 per bushel. Since it is expected that 100*3000 = 300,000 bushels will be produced, today's wheat price is $7. Assume the length of the growing season is six months and the risk-free rate is 5%. An increase in production by Farmer Jones (up to 5000 bushels) will increase his revenue. Increased production by Farmer Jones is associated with lower price. To hedge his risk, Farmer Jones would like to go long wheat futures. This is because being long wheat futures will benefit Farmer Jones as production decreases and price increases. Thus a good production year should result in high profit from the farm and low profit from the futures while a bad production year will result in low profit from the farm and high profit from the futures. Whether production is high or low, we have created a hedge by going long six month futures. The question is how many wheat futures to go long in order to minimize the standard deviation of total profit?

Figure 29.2

	A	B	C	D	E
1	**Corn**	P=10-Supply/100000			
2	Expected yield/acre	3000			Profit
3	expected price	7		Bushels	21547.75
4	interest rate	0.05		500	4870.247
5	length of season	0.5		1000	9227.836
6	Current futures price	7.177206		1500	13072.77
7	Yield/acre	3003.937		2000	16405.04
8	Total production	300393.7		2500	19224.66
9	Actual corn price in future	7.173169		3000	21531.62
10	Bushels long in futures	3998		3500	23325.92
11				4000	24607.56
12	Profit			4500	25376.55
13	Futures profit	-16.1403		5000	25632.88
14	Corn profit	21547.75		5500	25376.55
15	Total profit	21531.61		6000	24607.56
16					
17					
18				StdDev = 1396.7286	
19					

Solution

Note in column D and E our data table shows that farmer Jones' profit increases as production increases up to 5000 bushels and then decreases. We proceed as follows:

Step by Step

Step 1: In B6 we use (29.1) to compute today's wheat futures price

$=B3*EXP(B4*B5).$

Here we use the fact that today's wheat price is $7.

Step 2: In B7 we determine Farmer Jones' (random) production yield

$=RiskTnormal(3000,1000,0,15000).$

We use the truncated normal to exclude the possibility of negative demand.

Step 3: In B8 we compute total wheat production with the formula

$=100*B7.$

Step 4: In B9 we compute the actual wheat price at the end of the season. We assume that (due to inflation) today's demand curve will shift up by an amount $e^{.05(5)}$.

$=(10-B8/100000)*EXP(B4*B5).$

Step 5: In B10 we enter a trial number of wheat futures to go long.

Step 6: In cell B13 we compute our profit from the futures. By convergence, the price of our futures contract in six months will equal the spot price so our profit is given by

$$=(B9-B6)*B10.$$

Note that a higher price benefits us because we have gone long futures.

Step 7: In B14 we compute our revenue from corn sales as price*(production quantity) with the formula

$$=B9*B7.$$

Step 8: In cell B15 we compute total profit with the formula

$$=SUM(B13:B14).$$

Step 9: We now use RISKOptimizer to determine the standard deviation minimizing number of futures to purchase.

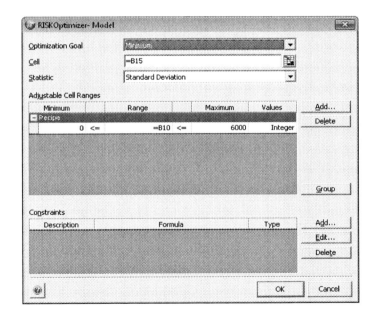

We minimize the standard deviation (cell B15) of total profit. We adjust number of futures (cell B10) we go long. We constrain the number of futures to be an integer between 0 and 6000. RISKOptimizer recommends going long 3998 bushels of futures. This will reduce our standard deviation to $1397. With no hedging our standard deviation would be $4227!

Reference
Luenberger, D., *Investment Science*, Oxford Press, 1997.

Chapter 30: Controlling VAR with Correlated Assets

Most investments are correlated. For example, most US stocks tend to go up and down with the market as a whole. This induces a correlation between the returns on various US stocks. Using RISKOptimizer we can easily maximize the VAR of a portfolio, given a constraint on expected return. To model the correlations between investments we use the RiskCorrmat function. Here is an illustration of how to use RISKOptimizer to control the VAR of a portfolio involving correlated assets.

Example 30.1 The annual return on each stock is assumed to follow a Lognormal random variable with the given value of μ and σ for each stock as well as the following correlations:

Figure 30.1

	A	B	C	D	E
9		Mu	Sigma	New Price	
10	Stock 1	0.15	0.2	1.13882838	
11	Stock 2	0.1	0.12	1.09724226	
12	Stock 3	0.25	0.4	1.18530485	
13	Stock 4	0.16	0.2	1.1502738	
14					
15	Correlation Matrix				
16		Stock 1	Stock 2	Stock 3	Stock 4
17	Stock 1	1	0.8	0.7	0.6
18	Stock 2	0.8	1	0.75	0.55
19	Stock 3	0.7	0.75	1	0.65
20	Stock 4	0.6	0.55	0.65	1

Suppose we want an expected return of at least 15% on our portfolio, but want to maximize our VAR. How should we allocate our assets?

Solution See file corr.xls. and Figure 30.2. The trick is to ensure that the stock prices a year from now are correlated.

Figure 30.2

	A	B	C	D	E
2					
3					
4	Fraction in		Current Price		
5	Stock 1	0.604067	$ 1.00		
6	Stock 2	0.238436	$ 1.00		
7	Stock 3	0.000191	$ 1.00		
8	Stock 4	0.157305	$ 1.00		
9		Mu	Sigma	New Price	
10	Stock 1	0.15	0.2	1.13882838	
11	Stock 2	0.1	0.12	1.09724226	
12	Stock 3	0.25	0.4	1.18530485	
13	Stock 4	0.16	0.2	1.1502738	
14					
15	Correlation Matrix				
16		Stock 1	Stock 2	Stock 3	Stock 4
17	Stock 1	1	0.8	0.7	0.6
18	Stock 2	0.8	1	0.75	0.55
19	Stock 3	0.7	0.75	1	0.65
20	Stock 4	0.6	0.55	0.65	1
21					
22	New Value	1.130722			
23	Portfolio retu	0.130722			
24					
25	Mean return	0.150228			
26				Percentile(0.05) = -.1293	
27					
28					

Step by Step

Step 1: Enter trial asset allocations in cells B5:B8. These need to add to one, because we will use the Budget method of solution. The Budget method will ensure that all simulations use asset allocations that add to one.

Step 2: We assume that each stock price follows a Lognormal random variable. From (26.1) it follows that to generate Stock 1 price a year from now enter into D10 the formula

$$=RiskCorrmat(\$B\$17:\$E\$20,1)+EXP((B10-0.5*C10\wedge2)+C10* RiskNormal(0,1)).$$

This ensures that Stock 1's price one Year from now will be correlated with Stocks 2-4 according to Column 1 of the numbers in B17:E20. Note that

$$EXP((B10-0.5*C10\wedge2)+C10*RiskNormal(0,1))$$

would generate the Stock 1 Price in absence of correlations.

In D11 generate Stock 2 price a year from now with formula

$=RiskCorrmat(\$B\$17{:}\$E\$20,2)+EXP((B11-0.5*C11^2)+C11* RiskNormal(0,1)).$

In D12 generate Stock 3 price a year from now with formula

$=RiskCorrmat(\$B\$17{:}\$E\$20,3)+EXP((B12-0.5*C12^2)+C12* RiskNormal(0,1))$

In D13 generate Stock 4 price a year from now with the formula

$=RiskCorrmat(\$B\$17{:}\$E\$20,4)+EXP((B13-0.5*C13^2)+C13* RiskNormal(0,1)).$

Step 3: In B22 we now compute the value of our portfolio one year from now with the formula

$=SUMPRODUCT(B5{:}B8,D10{:}D13).$

Step 4: In B23 we now compute the return on our portfolio with the formula

$=(B22/1)-1.$

Step 5: In cell B25 we compute the mean return on our portfolio for a given simulation with the formula

$=RiskMean(B23).$

Step 6: We can now use RISKOptimizer to maximize VAR, subject to an expected return of at least 15%. Our Settings box follows on the next page.

We choose to maximize the 5th percentile or VAR of the portfolio return (cell B23). We adjust our asset allocations (B5:B8) by the budget method. We constrain each asset allocation to be non-negative. This prohibits short selling. Our simulation constraint of RISKMEAN(B23)>=.15 ensures that each asset allocation considered yields an expected return of at least 15%. RISKOptimizer obtains a VAR of -12.93%. Our asset allocation is 60% to Stock 1, 24% to Stock 2 and 16% to Stock 4. Even though Stock 3 has highest mean return it is hardly used due to its high volatility. An average return of 15% (see cell B25) is attained.

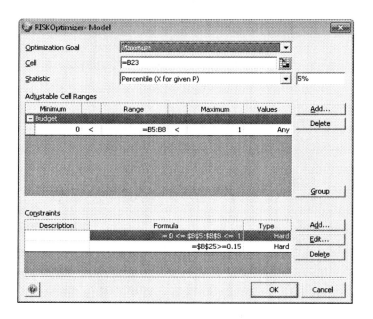

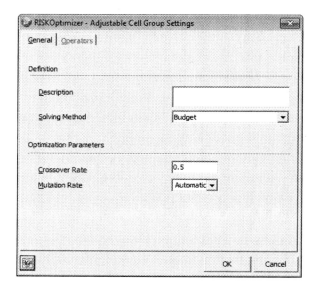

Chapter 31: An Introduction to Real Options: Modeling a Gold Mine Lease and Expansion

Suppose the uncertainty concerning an investment decision deals primarily with risk involving the price of a commodity. Then the risk neutral approach discussed in Chapter 25 implies (in our analysis we ignore convenience costs and storage yields) that an investment decision may be valued as the expected discounted (at risk-free rate) value of cash flows generated by the investment under the assumption that the price of the relevant commodity grows at the risk free rate. This is because in a risk neutral world the value of any asset must grow at the risk free rate. In the next two chapters we will use the real options approach to value three options involving a gold mine. Our inspiration comes from Chapter 12 of Luenberger (1997).

Example 31.1   Assume the current price of gold is $400 per ounce. The price of gold evolves through time as a Lognormal random variable with an annual volatility of 30%. The current risk-free rate is 10%. It costs $300 per ounce to extract gold, so we will only extract gold during a year in which the price exceeds $300. Up to 10,000 ounces of gold can be mined and sold each year. Assuming cash flows occur at the end of each year, value a 10 year lease on this gold mine.

Solution   Our work is in file gold1.xls. See Figure 31.1.

Step by Step   Step 1: We enter relevant parameters in B1:B5. We name cell B1 r_ and name B2 sigma.

Step 2: In B8:K8 we use (26.1) to generate gold prices (per ounce) for the next 10 years. *To perform a risk neutral valuation, we assume price of gold grows at risk free rate.* This is because in a risk neutral world, gold prices would grow (ignoring convenience yields and storage costs) at the risk free rate. In B8 we enter the current gold price $400. In C8:K8 we use (26.1) to generate future gold prices by copying from C8 to D8:K8 the formula

$$=B8*EXP((r\_-0.5*sigma^2)+sigma*RiskNormal(0,1)).$$

Figure 31.1

	A	B	C	D	E	F	G	H	I	J	K
1	r	0.1									
2	sigma	0.3									
3	extraction rate	10000									
4	current price	400									
5	ext cost	300									
6											
7	time	0	1	2	3	4	5	6	7	8	9
8	price	400	422.616	446.511	471.757	498.4307	526.612	556.387	587.85	621.08	656.2
9	mine?	yes	yes	yes	yes	yes	yes	yes	yes	yes	yes
10	profit		1000000	1226162	1465112	1717572	1984307	2266123	2563873	3E+06	3E+06	4E+06
11											
12											
13	npv	1.21E+07			Name	npv / yes					
14					Descriptio	Output					
15					Cell	B13					
16					Minimum	909090.9					
17					Maximum	1.63E+08					
18					Mean =	1.92E+07					

Step 3: In B9:K9 we indicate that we will mine gold if and only if price is greater than $300 per ounce. Simply copy from B9 to C9:K9 the formula

=IF(B8>$B$5,"yes","no").

Step 4: In B10:K10 we compute the annual profit from mining. If we do not mine profit is $0. If we mine we simply take extraction rate times profit earned per ounce extracted. Simply copy from B10 to C10:K10 the formula

=IF(B9="yes",$B$3*(B8-$B$5),0).

Step 5: In cell B13 we compute the discounted value (*at risk free rate, because that is proper discount rate in a risk neutral world!*) **of our profits with the formula**

=NPV(r_,B10:K10).

Step 6: Running an @RISK simulation we find (see cell F18) that the option to lease the gold mine is worth $19.2 million.

Valuing an Expansion Option

Let's assume that we can expand the capacity of the mine. If we expand the capacity of the mine we can extract 50% more gold per year, but extraction cost will increase by $20 per ounce. It will cost $8 million to expand the mine. By how much does this expansion option increase the value of the lease?

Solution

Our work is in Figure 31.2 and file gold2.xls. We need to have adjustable cells for each year that determine whether or not we should expand (assuming we have not already expanded). It can easily be shown that for each year t there exists a cutoff point p(t) such that we should expand if year t price is at least p(t) and not expand if year t price is less than p(t). We will use RISKOptimizer to find the cutoffs that maximize the expected discounted (at risk free rate) value of cash flows over 10 years. This problem could also be solved using binomial trees (see Chapter 56 of Winston (1998)).

Figure 31.2

	A	B	C	D	E	F	G	K
1		current	expansion					
2	r	0.1						
3	sigma	0.3						
4	extraction rate	10000	15000					
5	current price	400						
6	ext cost	300	320					
7	cost		8.00E+06					
8	time	0	1	2	3	4	5	9
9	price	400	469.83516	421.058	486.485	200.03	131.784	150.222
10	cut for expand?	1070	623	693	724	684	800	1882
11	expanded already?	no	no	no	no	no	no	no
12	expand now?	no	no	no	no	no	no	no
13	profit	1000000	1698351.6	1210581	1864854	0	0	0
14	buildingcost	0	0	0	0	0	0	0
15	profit	1000000	1698351.6	1210581	1864854	0	0	0
16	npv	4.50E+06						
17								
18								
19					Mean = 2.1638E+007			
20								

Step by Step

Step 1: Enter parameter values in rows 2-7 and generate gold prices for years 0-9 as before.

Step 2: In B10:K10 enter trial cutoff points for the p(t).

Step 3: In B11:K11 determine if we have already expanded. In B11 enter "no" because we have not yet expanded. In C11:K11 determine if by beginning of year we have already expanded by copying from C11 to D11:K11 the formula

   $=IF(OR(B11="yes",B12="yes"),"yes","no")$.

If we have already expanded at beginning of previous year or we expand during previous year, this formula enters a "yes", otherwise it enters a "no".

Step 4: In B12:K12 we determine if we expand during the current year. We expand if and only if we have not yet expanded and price of gold during current year exceeds cutoff . Simply copy from B12 to C12:K12 the formula

$$=IF(AND(B11="no",B9>=B10),"yes","no").$$

This formula ensures that we expand if and only if current price exceeds cutoff and we have not yet expanded.

Step 5: In B13:K13 we determine profit (excluding building cost) for each year. Note that if we have expanded and current price is at least $320 per ounce we will sell 15,000,000 ounces at current price and it will cost us $320 per ounce to produce the gold. If we have not expanded and current price is at least $300 we will sell 10,000,000 ounces at current price and it will cost us $300 an ounce to produce the gold. Otherwise, we extract no gold. Copying from B13 to C13:K13 the formula

$$=IF(OR(B11="yes",B12="yes"),MAX(0,\$C\$4*(B9-\$C\$6)),MAX(0,\$B\$4*(B9-\$B\$6)))$$

will determine the correct profit for each year.

Step 6: In B14:K14 we compute the expansion cost (if any) incurred during the current year. If we expand, a cost of $8 million is incurred, otherwise no cost is incurred. Copying from B14 to C14:K14 the formula

$$=IF(B12="yes",\$C\$7,0)$$

picks up the expansion cost for each year.

Step 7: In B15:K15 we compute profit for each year by subtracting expansion cost from mining profit. Just copy from B15 to C15: K15 the formula

$$=B13-B14.$$

Step 8: In cell B16 we compute the expected discounted (at risk free rate) value of profits from gold mine with the formula

$$=NPV(r\_,B15:K15).$$

Step 9: We can now use RISKOptimizer to find out the value of the lease with expansion option. Our Model window follows:

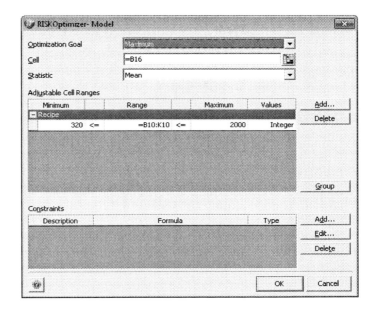

We try and choose the expansion cutoff points (B10:K10) to maximize the expected discounted NPV (cell B16) of profits. We constrain B10:K10 to be an integer between $320 and $2000. From Figure 31.2 we find that RISKOptimizer values this situation at $21.6 million. Thus the expansion option has increased the mine's value by $21.6 -$19.2 = $2.4 million.

Remark

The cutoffs p(t) found by RISKOptimizer may not be the exact cutoffs that maximize profit. If a particular p(t) does not have much effect on value of option, then RISKOptimizer will not expend much effort in accurately determining p(t). We can be fairly sure, however, that the value of the option found by RISKOptimizer is fairly close to the actual maximum expected discounted value that could be obtained by exhaustively searching all combinations of p(t)'s.

Chapter Remarks

The risk neutral approach can be used to value many real investment options such as expansion, contraction, and abandonment. A more comprehensive set of real options examples is given in Chapters 55-58 of Winston (1998).
1. The end of chapter references contain many other applications of real options.
2. The web site www.real-options.com contains a great deal of useful information on real options.

References

Amram, M. and Kulatilaka, N., *Real Options,* HBS Press, 1999.
Brealey, R. and Myers, S., *Principles of Corporate Finance*, Prentice-Hall 1996.
Luenberger, D., *Investment Science*, Oxford Press, 1997.
Nichols, N., "Scientific Management at Merck: An Interview with CFO Judy Lewent," *Harvard Business Review*, Vol. 72 No. 1, pages 89-99, 1994.
Trigeorgis, L., *Real Options*, MIT Press, 1996.
Trigeorgis, L., *Real Options in Capital Investment*, Praeger, 1995.
Winston, W., *Financial Models Using Simulation and Optimization*, Palisade, 1998.

Chapter 32: Modeling a Startup and Shutdown Option

We now extend the gold mine example of Chapter 31 to allow the mine owner to shut down the mine (to save fixed operating costs) when the price of gold is low and reopen the mine when the price of gold increases.

Example 32.1 We are interested in the value of owning a gold mine over the next 20 years. The current price of gold is $400 per ounce and the annual volatility is 30%. It costs $250 per ounce to extract an ounce of gold. In addition, a fixed cost of $1,000,000 is incurred each year the mine is open. After observing the price of gold for the year we may (for a cost of $1,500,000) shut down an open mine or (for a cost of $2,000,000) open a shut down mine. Use real options theory to value this situation. Assume the mine is open at the beginning of the problem.

Solution Our work is in the file goldshut.xls. See Figure 32.1. As in Chapter 31, we let gold price grow at the risk-free rate. Then we value the situation as the expected discounted (at risk-free rate) value of our profits given we act each year in a way that maximizes our expected NPV.

Figure 32.1

	A	B	C	D	E	F	G	T	U
1	r	0.1							
2	sigma	0.3							
3	extraction rate	10000							
4	current price	400							
5	ext cost	250							
6	fixed cost	1000000							
7	start up cost	2000000							
8	shutdown cost	1500000							
9									
10	time	0	1	2	3	4	5	18	19
11	price	400	1060.235	884.4431	1098.061	1310.676	1220.669	3832.948	5674.676
12	open at begining?	yes	yes	yes	yes	yes	yes	yes	yes
13	open cutoff		410	1909	502	401	368	385	400	1999
14	do we open?	no	no	no	no	no	no	no	no
15	shut cutoff		181	215	264	255	85	244	261	17
16	do we shut?	no	no	no	no	no	no	no	no
17	status?	yes	yes	yes	yes	yes	yes	yes	yes
18	nonextraction costs	1000000	1000000	1000000	1000000	1000000	1000000	1000000	1000000
19	extraction cash flows	1500000	8102353	6344431	8480608	10606756	9706694	35829479	54246763
20	total cash flows	500000	7102353	5344431	7480608	9606756	8706694	34829479	53246763
21	npv	$144,442,305.76							
22									
23									
24					Mean = 4.3479E+007				
25									

The key to our model is to have "cutoff" prices of gold for each year which determine when we open a shut mine or close an open mine. In Row 13 we have an Adjustable cell O(t) for each year. If price of gold during year t is at least O(t) we open a shut mine. In Row 15 we have an Adjustable cell S(t) for each year. If price of gold during year t is less than or equal to S(t) we will shut down an open mine. The rest of the spreadsheet is simple bookkeeping. Note that we will mine gold with open mine if and only if per ounce gold price is more than $250.

Step by Step **Step 1: In A1:B8 we enter problem parameters.**

Step 2: In B11:U11 we use the Lognormal random variable (as described in Chapter 31) to generate 20 years of random gold prices.

Step 3: In B13:U13 we enter trial values of the O(t), price cutoffs for opening a shut mine.

Step 4: In B15:U15 we enter trial values of the S(t), price cutoffs for closing an open mine.

Step 5: In Row 12 we will keep track of whether the mine is open at the beginning of the year. See Step 9.

Step 6: In B14:U14 we determine if a shut mine was opened during the year. To do this copy the statement

=IF(AND(B12="no",B11>=B13),"yes","no")

from B14 to C14:U14. This ensures that the mine will be opened during year t if year t gold price is at least O(t) and mine was closed at end of last year.

Step 7: In B16:U16 we determine if an open mine is shut down during the current year. To do this copy the statement

=IF(AND(B12="yes",B11<=B15),"yes","no")

from B16 to C16:U16

Step 8: In B17:U17 we determine the status of the mine at the end of the year by copying from B17 to C17:U17 the formula

=IF(B14="yes","yes",IF(B16="yes","no",IF(AND(B12="yes",B16="no"),"yes","no"))).

If the mine is opened during the current year, this formula generates a "yes". If the mine is closed during the current year, this formula generates a "no". If the mine was open at the beginning of the year and was not shut, this formula generates a "yes". Otherwise the mine is closed and the formula generates a "no".

Step 9: In B12:U12 we generate the status of the mine at the beginning of each year. In B12 we enter a "yes" because mine starts open. In C12:U12 we just recopy the status at the end of the previous year by copying from C12 to D12:U12 the formula

=B17.

Step 10: In B18:U18 we generate the fixed operating costs, start-up costs, and shut-down costs for each year by copying from B18 to C18:U18 the formula

=IF(B17="yes",$B$6,0)+IF(B14="yes",$B$7,0)+IF(B16="yes",$B$8,0).

The first =IF statement incurs a fixed cost if mine is operating. The second =IF statement incurs a startup cost if we open the mine. The third =IF statement incurs a shutdown cost if we close the mine.

Step 11: In B19:U19 we compute the extraction cash flows for each year. Note that we will mine to capacity if and only if mine is open and current price of gold is more than $250. Simply copy from B19 to C19:U19 the formula

=IF(B17="yes",MAX(0,(B11-$B$5)*$B$3),0).

If we are open we extract our capacity if gold price exceeds $250 and earn (gold price - 250) per ounce extracted. Otherwise we earn nothing.

Step 12: By copying from B20 to C20:U20 the formula

=B19-B18

we compute our profit for each year.

Step 13: In cell B21 we compute the NPV (at risk-free rate) of our profits with the formula (we named risk-free rate r_)

=NPV(r_,B20:U20).

Step 14: We are ready to use RISKOptimizer to choose gold price cutoffs that maximize our expected discounted NPV. Our Model window follows:

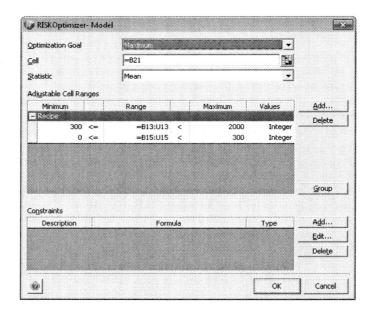

We are trying to maximize mean NPV (cell B21). Our Adjustable Cell Ranges are price cutoffs for opening the mine (B13:U13) and price cutoffs for shutting the mine (B15:U15). We constrain the price cutoffs for opening to be between $0 and $2000. We constrain the price cutoffs for shutting to be at most $300. RISKOptimizer reports that the value of owning this mine for 20 years is $43.5 million.

Remark

Again, we have ignored storage costs and convenience yields in our analysis.

Chapter 33: Timing Market Entry

When a high-tech company is trying to determine whether to market a new product there is a great deal of uncertainty. Should we enter the market now, not knowing if growth in the market will be high or low? If we enter now, we get a larger market share than we would get by entering later. The downside is we may have a high share of a small market. If we wait a few years, we will know if market growth will be high or low, but we have missed out on several years of sales and will probably obtain a reduced market share due to our late entry. RISKOptimizer can be used to make these complex entry decisions. The following example explores some of the important issues involved in the decision to enter a market.

Example 33.1 Fell Computers is trying to determine whether to enter a market for a new type of computer. They can enter the market now or wait two years and enter the market at the beginning of Year 3. It will cost $3.5 billion to enter this market in Year 3 and $3 billion to enter this market in Year 1. Year 1 market size is unknown but is believed to follow a normal random variable with mean 5,000,000 and standard deviation 1,000,000. There are three scenarios for market growth: High, Medium, and Low. Relevant information for each scenario is given below:

Scenario	Unit profit contribution	Market size growth years 2-6	Market size growth after year 6	Probability of scenario
High	$90	μ = 100% σ = 20%	μ = 15% σ = 20%	.1
Medium	$60	μ = 20% σ = 15%	μ = 5% σ = 15%	.5
Low	$40	μ = -5% σ = 15%	μ = -20% σ = 15%	.4

For example, the High scenario is estimated to have a 10% chance of occurring. If the High scenario occurs a unit profit of $90 can be earned on each sale. Annual growth during Years 2-6 will follow a normal distribution with mean 100% and standard deviation 20%. After Year 6, the product will reach the mature portion of the product life cycle and grow annually according to a normal random variable with mean 15% and standard deviation of 20%.

If we enter the market now our market share is equally likely to assume any value between 30% and 50%. Each year our market share will on average equal the previous year's market share with a standard deviation equal to 10% of the previous year's share. If we wait two years before entering our market share is equally likely to assume any value between 20% and 40%. As before, each year our market share will on average equal the previous year's market share with a standard deviation equal to 10% of the previous year's share.

Fell is trying to determine whether to enter the market now or wait two years and decide. Their goal is to maximize the mean NPV of their decision over 20 years. A 20% risk adjusted discount rate has been deemed appropriate for the project. What should Fell do?

Solution

To model this problem with RISKOptimizer we will use two Adjustable cells:

- A 0-1 cell that indicates whether we enter now or not. A "1" will indicate Year 1 entry. A "0" will indicate no Year 1 entry.
- An integer cell that represents a threshold point T for Year 2 demand that drives our Year 3 entry decision. If we have not already entered and Year 2 demand is at least T we enter during Year 3, otherwise we do not enter during Year 3.

Our work is in file newtech.xls. See Figure 33.1.

Figure 33.1

	A	B	C	D	E	F	G	H	I	U
1	New Technology									
2										
3	Year	1	2	3	4	5	6	7	8	20
4	Enter now?	0	0	0	0	0	0	0	0	0
5	Year 2 cutoff for entry		6.62E+06							
6	Fixed cost	0		0	0	0	0	0	0	0
7	Scenario	2	2	2	2	2	2	2	2	2
8	Market Size	3739181.901	3793917	5121865	6893461	8068310	11444055	13871282	12439732	23969083
9	Market Share	0	0	0	0	0	0	0	0	0
10	Unit Margin	60	60	60	60	60	60	60	60	60
11	Profit	0	0	0	0	0	0	0	0	0
12	NPV	0.00E+00								
13										
14										
15										
16			Mean = 1.5388E+009							

Through judicious use of IF statements we will ensure that the spreadsheet models the entry decision to be consistent with the previous definition of our adjustable cells.

Step 1: In B4 enter a trial value (0 or 1) for the Year 1 entry decision. In cell C5 enter a trial value for the Year 2 demand cutoff which will generate a Year 3 entry. In cell D4 we indicate if an entry occurs during Year 3 with the formula

=IF(AND(B4=0,C8>=C5),1,0).

This formula ensures that Year 3 entry occurs if and only if Year 1 entry does not occur and Year 2 demand exceeds cutoff.

Step 2: In cells B6 and D6 we generate the entry cost (if any). Year 1 entry cost is generated in cell B6 with the formula

=IF(B4=1,3000000000,0).

Year 3 entry cost is generated in cell D6 with the formula

=IF(D4=1,3500000000,0).

Entry cost is $0 in all other years.

Step 3: In row 7 we generate the demand scenario. Of course, when we make our decisions we do not know which demand scenario has transpired. In cell B7 we generate the demand scenario (1 = High, 2 = Medium, 3 = Low) with the formula

=RiskDiscrete({1,2,3},{0.1,0.5,0.4}).

Entering

=B7

in C7 and copying that formula to D7:U7 ensures that the same demand scenario is used to generate market size for each year.

Step 4: In cell B8 we generate Year 1 market size with the formula

=RiskNormal(5000000,1000000).

In cell C8 we generate Year 2 market size with the formula

=IF(B7=1,B8*RiskNormal(2,0.2),IF(B7=2,B8*RiskNormal(1.2,0.15),B8*RiskNormal(0.95,0.15))).

This formula grows the market according to the growth rate associated with the demand scenario that has actually occurred. Copying this formula to D8:G8 generates demand for years 3-6.

In cell H8 we generate Year 7 demand with the formula

=IF(G7=1,G8*RiskNormal(1.15,0.2),IF(G7=2,G8*RiskNormal(1.05,0.15),G8* RiskNormal(0.8,0.15))).

Copying this formula to I8:U8 models the slowdown in market growth due to product maturity.

Step 5: In cell B9 we use the =RiskUniform function to model our Year 1 market share (assuming a year 1 entry).

=IF($B4=1,RiskUniform(0.3,0.5),0).

Our Year 2 market share is computed in C9 with the formula

IF($B4=1,RiskNormal(1,0.1)*B9,0).

Our Year 3 market share is computed in D9 with the formula

=IF($B4=1,C9*RiskNormal(1,0.1),IF($D4=1,RiskUniform(0.2,0.4),0)).

This formula ensures that if Year 1 entry occurred, we modify our Year 2 market share. If Year 3 entry occurs, our share is equally likely to be between 30% and 50%. Otherwise we have no market share.

Finally, copying from E9 to F9:U9 the formula

=IF($B4=1,D9*RiskNormal(1,0.1),IF($D4=1,D9*RiskNormal(1,0.1),0)).

generates our market share for Years 4-20.

Step 6: In B10:U10 we compute the unit profit margin associated with the demand scenario by copying from B10 to C10:U10 the formula

=IF(B7=1,90,IF(B7=2,60,40)).

Step 7: In B11:U11 we compute each year's profit by copying the formula

=B10*B9*B8-B6

from B11 to C11:U11. For each year this formula computes

(market size)(market share)*(unit profit contribution) - building costs.*

Step 8: In cell B12 we compute our 20 year NPV (assuming end of year cash flows and a 20% discount rate) with the formula

=NPV(0.2,B11:U11).

Step 9: We are now ready to use RISKOptimizer to determine an optimal decision strategy. Our Model window follows:

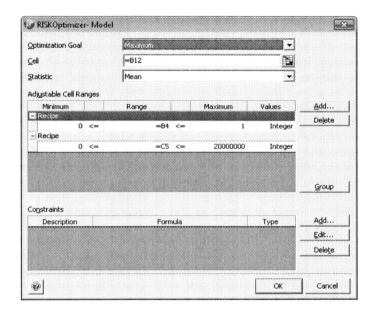

We choose to maximize mean NPV (cell B12) by adjusting our Year 1 entry decision (a 0-1 adjustable cell in B4) and our Year 2 entry threshold (cell C5). We constrain our Year 2 entry threshold to be an integer between 0 and 20,000,000. RISKOptimizer recommends not entering now. If Year 2 demand is at least 6.62 million, then Fell should enter the market. Otherwise do not enter the market. An expected NPV of around $1.53 billion is associated with this strategy.

Chapter 34: Test-Marketing a New Product

Major consumer goods firms often test market a new product before taking the product nationwide. The reasoning is that the small cost of test marketing usually gives the company a good idea about how well the product will do nationwide. Thus test marketing can often prevent a costly national failure. An important decision in test marketing a new product is how well the product must do in the test market to justify a national rollout. The following example shows how RISKOptimizer can be used to make test-marketing decisions.

Example 34.1   Q and H is a large consumer goods corporation. They are thinking of marketing a new barbecue sauce nationwide. In the past many products have been test marketed and then rolled out nationally. Figure 34.1 (see file tm.xls) gives the following information about 19 of Q and H's products:

- A consensus forecast for annual national sales of each product. This forecast was made before test marketing took place.
- A forecast for annual national sales made after test marketing took place.
- Actual national sales of the product.

For the new product a test market study will cost $90,000. The consensus view (before test marketing) is that annual sales will equal 510,000 units. The cost of nationally rolling out the product is estimated at $3.2 million. Each unit sells for $4.00 and costs $3.20 to produce. We believe the product will sell for ten years. What strategy maximizes the expected NPV from the product? Assume a discount rate of 10%.

Figure 34.1

	A	B	C
1	Consenus	Test Forecast	Actual
2	559502	271368.84	267987.2802
3	964473	1047337.5	1138569.115
4	984187	856605.85	780247.0422
5	443883	393328.39	372377.1092
6	704814	659044.38	663591.9186
7	220327	279390.47	290172.0839
8	192038	149118.68	140381.2244
9	453347	389535.8	380996.8252
10	321447	210441.36	203257.2687
11	225307	57193.205	45358.6171
12	120672	56415.471	66285.21426
13	362419	186467.23	196948.7063
14	935354	943745.02	956951.0151
15	285593	355474.82	391143.9342
16	772230	668936.89	698553.0442
17	242632	162547.32	178234.6341
18	379353	260883.89	295805.7821
19	952275	1072461.4	1236328.678
20	629192	588194.84	635897.1059

Solution

We begin by trying to estimate three uncertain relationships:

- The relationship between the consensus forecast and actual sales.
- The relationship between the consensus forecast and the test marketing forecast.
- The relationship between the test market forecast and actual sales.

The techniques developed in Chapter 7 will be used to model these relationships. Then we develop a spreadsheet model to determine whether or not to test market and whether or not to roll the product out nationally. Our model will use the following adjustable cells:

- A 0-1 adjustable cell which tells us (if a "1") that we test market and (if a "0") that we do not test market.
- A cell containing a cutoff point T such that if forecast for national sales after test marketing is at least T we should market nationally, otherwise do not market nationally.
- A cell containing a cutoff point T' such that if we do not test market, we will market nationally if consensus forecast is at least T', and we do not market nationally if consensus forecast is less than T'.

We begin by estimating the relationship between the consensus forecast and actual sales. See Figure 34.2.

Figure 34.2

	D	E	F	G
1		Actual/ Consensus	Unbiased CF	Actual/UBC
2		0.47897466	476108.1	0.56287069
3		1.18050906	820718	1.38728415
4		0.79278332	837493.7	0.93164532
5		0.83890825	377722.1	0.98584937
6		0.94151353	599761.3	1.10642675
7		1.31700647	187487.2	1.54769011
8		0.73100753	163414.7	0.85904903
9		0.84040884	385775.5	0.9876128
10		0.63231969	273535.2	0.74307527
11		0.20131916	191724.9	0.23658174
12		0.5493007	102685.8	0.64551487
13		0.5434282	308400.3	0.63861376
14		1.02308967	795939.2	1.20229156
15		1.36958516	243025.3	1.60947836
16		0.90459195	657128.9	1.06303808
17		0.73458832	206467.6	0.86325702
18		0.77976392	322810.3	0.91634547
19		1.29828955	810338.1	1.52569478
20		1.01065669	535410.8	1.18768086
21	mean	0.85094972		1
22	stdev	0.30654985		0.36024438

Step by Step

Step 1: For each product we determine the ratio of the actual sales to the consensus forecast by copying from E2 to E3:E20 the formula

=C2/A2.

Averaging these numbers in E21 shows us actual sales average out to 85% of consensus forecast. Thus, unsurprisingly, the marketing department has tended to over-forecast sales.

Step 2: To correct for this bias, we create unbiased forecasts by multiplying each consensus forecast by .8509. To do this copy the formula

=$E$21*A2

from F2 to F3:F20.

Step 3: In G2:G20 we analyze the percentage errors for our unbiased forecasts by computing the ratio of actual sales to our unbiased forecasts. Simply copy from G2 to G3:G20 the formula

=C2/F2

from G2 to G3:G20. Unsurprisingly we find (in G21) that the ratio of actual to unbiased forecast average out to one. The standard deviation of these ratios is .36.

Assuming normality, we can now model actual sales as a normal random variable with

Mean =.85*(consensus forecast) (34.1)

Standard Deviation = .36*.85*(original consensus forecast).

In a similar fashion (see Figure 34.3) we find that actual sales can be modeled as a normal random variable with

Mean = 1.03*(test market forecast) (34.2)

Standard Deviation = .09*1.03*(original forecast from test marketing).

Figure 34.3

	H	I	J
1	**Actual/TF**	**Unbiased TF for Actual**	**Actual/UTF for Actual**
2	0.98753887	278655.5862	0.961715083
3	1.087108096	1075460.441	1.05868061
4	0.91085888	879607.2605	0.887040248
5	0.946733357	403889.97	0.92197662
6	1.006900194	676740.9166	0.980570115
7	1.038589778	286892.6064	1.011431028
8	0.941406044	153122.7835	0.916788614
9	0.978079108	399995.5368	0.952502691
10	0.965861797	216092.089	0.940604858
11	0.793077029	58728.94584	0.77233835
12	1.174947468	57930.32783	1.144223013
13	1.056210796	191474.2167	1.028591263
14	1.01399318	969086.2799	0.987477622
15	1.100342174	365019.959	1.071568621
16	1.044273462	686899.0555	1.016966086
17	1.096509245	166912.0044	1.067835922
18	1.133859885	267889.0977	1.104209856
19	1.152795517	1101258.911	1.122650328
20	1.081099434	603988.9311	1.052829072
21	1.026851806	465244.4694	1
22	0.093513861	341059.7993	0.091068507

In a similar fashion (see Figure 34.4) we find that the test market forecast may be modeled as a normal random variable with

Mean = .82*(consensus forecast)   **(34.3)**

Standard Deviation = .33*.82*(consensus forecast).

Figure 34.4

	K	L	M
		Unbiased	**Actual**
1	**TF/Consensus**	**Cons for TF**	**TF/UC for TF**
2	0.4850185 39	45924 5.8114	0.5909 0 1073
3	1.0859169 06	79165 0.7635	1.322979 254
4	0.8703689 91	80783 2.2462	1.060375 902
5	0.8861082 59	36434 4.3786	1.079551 148
6	0.9350614 27	57851 9.6073	1.139191 094
7	1.2680718 56	18084 6.9887	1.544899 751
8	0.7765060 96	15762 7.0454	0.946022 158
9	0.8592442 37	37211 2.5409	1.046822 545
10	0.6546689 14	26384 7.4721	0.797587 169
11	0.2538456 64	18493 4.6312	0.309261 735
12	0.4675 1086	99048.99457	0.56957 136
13	0.5145073 37	29747 7.7708	0.626827 457
14	1.0089709 58	76774 9.5464	1.229235 531
15	1.2446902 35	23441 8.0879	1.516413 777
16	0.8662404 88	63385 5.4518	1.05534 612
17	0.6699335 43	19915 5.1947	0.816184 161
18	0.6877074 76	31137 7.3969	0.837838 252
19	1.1262097 46	78163 8.5019	1.372068 268
20	0.9348415 71	51644 8.1818	1.138923 242
21	0.8208117 42	42116 4.7691	1
22	0.2726294 04	24106 5.5326	0.332146 082

We are now ready to set up our model for determining whether or not to test market and, if we test market, how to decide if we should go ahead nationally. See Figure 34.5.

Step by Step

Step 1: In B23 enter the consensus forecast for annual sales (510,000).

Step 2: In B26 we enter a trial value (0 or 1) for the 0-1 adjustable cell that determine whether or not we test market.

Figure 34.5

	A	B	C	D	E	F	G	H
23	Consensus forecast	510000						
24	1=Yes				Actual		Test forecast	
25	0 = No				Mean=.85*consensus		Mean=.82 consensus	
26	Test Market?	1			Sigma=.36*mean		Std dev=.33*mean	
27	Forecasted test mark	418200			Actual			
28	Actual test Market	272225.38			Mean=1.03*actual test market			
29	Forecast for actual	280392.14			Sigma=.09*mean			
30	Actual sales	273935.84						
31								
32	Cutoff no test	691345						
33	Cutoff test	400000						
34	Go ahead?	0						
35	TM Cost	90000						
36	Product Life	10						
37	Development Cost	3.20E+06						
38	Price	$4.00						
39	VC	$3.20						
40	PV analysis							
41	revenues	0.00E+00						
42	VC	0.00E+00						
43	DC	0.00E+00						
44	TM Cost	9.00E+04						
45	Present Value	-9.00E+04						
46								
47								
48				Mean = 269257.6322				
49								

Step 3: In cell B27 we compute a predicted mean (given consensus forecast) for the test market forecast using (34.3).

$=IF(B26=0,"none",0.82*B23).$

Step 4: In B28 we use (34.3) to compute the actual test market forecast with the formula

$=IF(B27="none","none",RiskNormal(B27,0.33*B27)).$

Step 5: In B29 we compute a forecast for the mean of actual sales(based on either the consensus or test market results) with the formula

$=IF(B26=1,1.03*B28,0.85*B23).$

If we test market our forecast for actual annual sales is *1.03*test market forecast* while if we do not test market our best guess for actual annual sales is *.85*consensus forecast.*

Step 6: In cell B30 we generate actual annual sales with the formula

$=IF(B26=1,RiskNormal(B29,B29*0.09),RiskNormal(B29,0.36*B29)).$

If we test market, actual annual sales are generated using (34.2). If we do not test market actual annual sales are generated with (34.1).

Step 7: In cell B32 we enter a trial value for the cutoff for unbiased consensus forecast. Let's assume we do not test market. If the unbiased consensus forecast is greater than or equal to this cutoff we will go national; if the unbiased consensus forecast is below this cutoff we will not go national.

Step 8: In cell B33 we enter a trial value for the cutoff for unbiased test market forecast. Let's assume we test market. If the unbiased test market forecast is greater than or equal to this cutoff we will go national; if the unbiased test market forecast is below this cutoff we will not go national.

Step 9: In B34 we determine if we go national with the product with the formula

=IF(AND(B26=1,B29>=B33),1,IF(AND(B26=0,B29>=B32),1,0)).

The first AND part of the IF statement ensures we go national if we test market and unbiased forecast from test marketing is at least as large as cutoff. The second AND part of statement ensures we go national if we do not test market and unbiased consensus forecast is at least as large as cutoff. Otherwise, we do not market nationally.

Step 10: In B35 we enter the test marketing cost ($90,000) and in B36 enter product life (10 years). In cell B37 we enter cost of a national rollout ($3.2 million). In B38 and B39 we enter unit price ($4.00) and variable cost ($3.20).

Step 11: In B41 we compute the NPV of revenues. Assuming revenues are received at end of year, the correct formula is

=IF(B34=0,0,(B38)*B30)*(-PV(0.1,B36,1).

The PV part of the formula computes NPV of $1 received at end of years 1, 2, …10, when discount rate is 10%. Note that if we do not roll product out nationally no revenue is received.

Step 12: In a similar fashion, we compute in B42 the NPV of variable costs with the formula

=IF(B34=0,0,B39*B30)*(-PV(0.1,B36,1)).

Step 13: In B43 we compute (assuming rollout cost is equally spread over product life) the NPV of the product rollout cost with the formula

=IF(B34=0,0,B37/10)*(-PV(0.1,B36,1)).

Again, this cost is incurred if and only if we go national.

Step 14: In B44 we incur test marketing cost (if any) with the formula

=IF(B26=1,B35,0).

Step 15: In B45 we compute the total NPV of the product with the formula

=B41-B42-B43-B44.

Step 16: We are now ready to use RISKOptimizer to determine the optimal strategy. Our Model window follows:

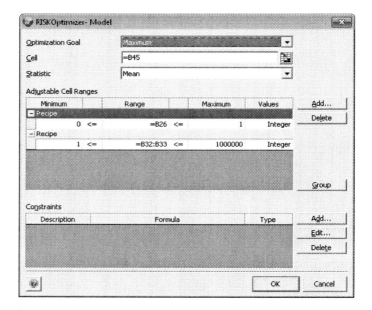

We choose to maximize mean NPV (cell B45) by adjusting the test market decision (cell B26) and our non-test marketing cutoff (B32) and test marketing cutoff (B33). We constrain our test market adjustable cell to equal 0 or 1 and allow our cutoffs to be any integer between 0 and 1,000,000. RISKOptimizer recommends test marketing and using a cutoff point of 400,000. Therefore, if our test market indicates annual sales of 400,000 units or more go ahead with a national rollout, otherwise do not roll out product nationally. This strategy yields an expected NPV of $269,257. Note the cutoff point for going national based on consensus forecast is not relevant because we choose to test market.

What about if Decision-Maker is Risk Averse?

In Chapter 22 we discussed how a utility function could be used to model the risk preferences of a risk-averse decision-maker. Let's suppose Q and H was risk-averse and had a utility function given by u(x) = Ln (x + 2,000,000), where x = NPV of project. This is a concave function, and therefore exhibits risk aversion. The only change in the model (see file tm2.xls and Figure 34.6) is to compute in cell B46 the utility with the formula

$$=LN(B45+2000000).$$

Then we adjust RISKOptimizer to maximize the mean of cell B46.

Figure 34.6

	A	B	C	D
23	Consensus forecast	510000		
24	1=Yes			
25	0 = No			
26	Test Market?	1		
27	Forecasted test market	418200		
28	Actual test Market	418200		
29	Forecast for actual	430746		
30	Actual sales	430746		
31				
32	Cutoff no test	379689		
33	Cutoff test	418192		
34	Go ahead?	1		
35	TM Cost	90000		
36	Product Life	10		
37	Development Cost	3.20E+06		
38	Price	$4.00		
39	VC	$3.20		
40	PV analysis			
41	revenues	1.06E+07		
42	VC	8.47E+06		
43	DC	1.97E+06		
44	TM Cost	9.00E+04		
45	Present Value	6.11E+04		
46	Utility	14.53876818		
47				
48				
49				Mean = 14.6238
50				

RISKOptimizer still recommends test marketing. Note that the cutoff point for the national rollout has increased to 418,192. This is because a risk averse decision-maker (as compared to as risk neutral decision maker) will require a more favorable assessment of the situation before going ahead with a risky expenditure.

Chapter 35: Stopping Rule Problems

Consider the following four situations in which a decision must be made in an uncertain environment.

- We are looking for a parking space near the movie theatre. Do we take an open space or proceed forward and look for a better space?
- We are looking for a new job. A job offer with an $80,000 salary is received. Do we accept this offer or search (at some cost) for a better offer?
- Amanda McBeal is marooned on a desert island. There are 1000 men on the island and she is allowed to choose her mate for life. She interviews each man one at a time. After interviewing each man she must decide whether to choose him or go on. She is not allowed to go back and select a man after she fails to choose him. At some point, she should select the best man she has seen so far. When does this point occur?
- We receive a $110,000 offer for our house that has been appraised at $115,000. Should we accept the offer or wait for a better offer?

All these examples are special cases of *stopping rule problems*. In a stopping rule problem we can "stop" the problem at any time and receive a known payoff or go on and receive a random payoff. The trick is to come up with a stopping rule that maximizes our expected payoff. If we combine RISKOptimizer with clever use of IF statements we can easily solve stopping rule problems. The following example highlights the basic ideas.

Example 35.1   Billie is taking Georgia to the movies, and wants to park as close as possible to the theatre. Billie estimates that there is a 12% chance that each parking space is empty. He approaches from the east and is wondering which parking place he should take in order to minimize the expected distance they will have to walk to the movie. Assume Billie can only see the current space and there are 15 spaces east of the movie theatre.

Solution   We will number parking spaces east of the movie as negative, spaces west of the movie as positive, and the theatre as 0. Our work is in file parking.xls. See Figure 35.1.

Figure 35.1

	A	B	C	D	E	F	G
1	Parking						
2	prob empty	0.12					
3	Take if closer than	-5					
4				payoff	3		
5	Space #	Empty?	Parked Yet?	Take Space?	Payoff		
6	-15	0	No	No	0		Mean = 5.9867
7	-14	0	No	No	0		
8	-13	1	No	No	0		
9	-12	0	No	No	0		
10	-11	0	No	No	0		
11	-10	0	No	No	0		
12	-9	0	No	No	0		
13	-8	0	No	No	0		
14	-7	0	No	No	0		
15	-6	0	No	No	0		
16	-5	0	No	No	0		
17	-4	0	No	No	0		
18	-3	1	No	Yes	3		
19	-2	0	Yes	No	0		
20	-1	0	Yes	No	0		
21	0	0	Yes	No	0		
22	1	0	Yes	No	0		
23	2	0	Yes	No	0		
24	3	0	Yes	No	0		
25	4	0	Yes	No	0		

A reasonable policy to follow is a *stopping rule* which takes the first open space after P* (including P*). For example, if P* = -7 Billie would park at the first open space among spaces -7, -6, ...0, 1, ... With a .12 chance of an empty space it is almost certain that Billie would find a space before reaching space 50, so we will truncate our spreadsheet after Billie looks at space 50. The key to the spreadsheet is to ensure that if Billie has taken a space, he cannot take another space, and to make sure that Billie takes the first empty space at or after P*.

Step by Step

Step 1: In B2 enter probability (.12) of empty space and in B3 enter trial value for P*.

Step 2: In cells A6:A71 we enter the parking space numbers, -15, -14, ...0, 1, 2, ... 50.

Step 3: In B6:B71 we determine which spaces are empty by copying the formula

$=RiskBinomial(1,\$B\$2)$

from B6 to B7:B71. This works because each space is a binomial random variable with one trial and a probability .12 of a success (an empty space). A "1" will then denote an empty space.

Step 4: In C6:C71 we determine if Billie has already parked before looking at the current space. We enter a No in C6 because he has seen no spaces. In C7:C71 we copy from C7 to C8:C71 the formula

$=IF(C6="Yes","Yes",IF(D6="Yes","Yes","No"))$.

If we have already taken a space or we take the space right before the current space this formula ensures that we have already taken a space. If we have not taken a space prior to seeing the current space a "no" is entered.

Step 5: In D6:D71 we determine if the current space will be taken by copying from D6 to D7:D71 the formula

$=IF(AND(B7=1,C7="No",A7>=\$B\$3),"Yes","No")$.

This formula takes the current space if and only if

- The space is empty.
- We have not yet taken a space.
- The space occurs at P* or after.

Step 6: In E6:E71 we determine the "payoff" associated with the current space. If we do not take the current space there is no payoff. If we take the current space, our payoff equals the absolute value of the current space. Thus our payoff may be computed by copying from E6 to E7:E71 the formula

$=IF(D6="Yes",ABS(A6),0)$.

Note only one number in column E will be non-zero, and that number is our total payoff.

Step 7: In E4 we compute our total payoff with the formula

$=SUM(E6:E71)$.

Step 8: **We can now use RISKOptimizer to determine the stopping rule that minimizes expected distance from the theatre.** Our Model window follows:

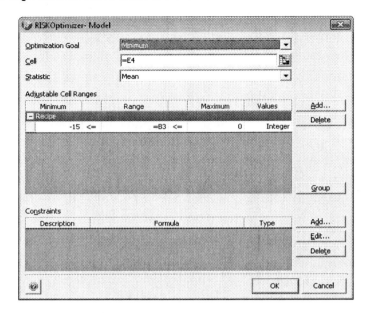

Our goal is to minimize expected distance from the theatre (cell E4). P* (cell B2) is our adjustable cell. We constrain P* to be an integer between -15 and 0. This is because Billie will clearly want to take (if he has not already parked) the first spot west of the theatre. RISKOptimizer recommends P* = -5. Thus once Billie is 5 spaces east of the theatre he should take the first open space. On average, Billie and Georgia will end up 5.99 spaces from the theatre.

Chapter 36: Maximizing Long-Term Growth: The Kelly Criteria

Suppose that at the beginning of each time period (say a year) you have n investments to which you may allocate money. Let X_0 = your initial capital and X_t = your capital at the end of period t. Then the t period growth rate is given by

$$\left(\frac{X_t}{X_0}\right)^{1/t}$$

At the beginning of each year, what fraction of your money should you allocate to each investment in order to maximize the expected long-term growth of your money? Kelly (1956) solved this problem. In order to maximize the expected long-term growth rate you should allocate your money among the n investments to maximize $E(Ln(R))$ where R = the *one-period* (random) return on your investment. If m = maximum $E(Ln(R))$, then the average per period rate at which your capital will grow is $e^m - 1$. *The importance of the Kelly criteria is that it reduces a complex multiple period problem to a simple one period optimization problem.*

We now apply the Kelly Growth criteria to the retirement example of Chapter 22.

Example 36.1   Attorney Amanda McBeal is saving for retirement. Each year she plans to allocate the same percentage of her assets to T-bills, bonds and stocks. What asset allocation will maximize the expected long-run growth rate (in terms of today's dollars) of her investments?

Solution   Our work is shown in Figures 36.1 and 36.2. (see file kelley.xls).

Figure 36.1

	A	B	C	D	E
3	Year	Bills	Bonds	Stocks	Inflation
4	1926	3.27	7.77	11.62	-1.49
5	1927	3.12	8.93	37.49	-2.08
6	1928	3.24	0.1	43.61	-0.97
7	1929	4.75	3.42	-8.42	0.19
8	1930	2.41	4.66	-24.9	-6.03
9	1931	1.07	-5.31	-43.34	-9.52
10	1932	0.96	16.84	-8.19	-10.3
11	1933	0.3	-0.08	53.99	0.51
12	1934	0.16	10.02	-1.44	2.03
13	1935	0.17	4.98	47.67	2.99
14	1936	0.18	7.51	33.92	1.21
15	1937	0.31	0.23	-35.03	3.1
16	1938	-0.02	5.53	31.12	-2.78
17	1939	0.02	5.94	-0.41	-0.48
18	1940	0	6.09	-9.78	0.96
19	1941	0.06	0.93	-11.59	9.72
20	1942	0.27	3.22	20.34	9.29
21	1943	0.35	2.08	25.9	3.16
22	1944	0.33	2.81	19.75	2.11

Figure 36.1 shows annual returns and inflation during the years 1926-1944 (we will use 1926-1994 in our analysis). For example, in 1926 T-bills yielded 3.27%, bonds yielded 7.77%, stocks yielded 11.62% and prices went down by 1.49%. We name the range (A4:E72) containing the asset returns and inflation for 1926-1994 Lookup.

We now simulate one year of investment. We use the =RISKDUNIFORM function to randomly choose a year from 1926-1994 as our scenario. Then we keep track of how the value of Amanda's portfolio has changed. Then we keep track of inflation each year and convert Amanda's final cash position into today's dollars. Suppose Amanda invests $1 today. According to the Kelley criteria, Amanda should allocate her assets in a way that maximizes the expected value of the logarithm of her portfolio's value after one year (measured in today's dollars).

Figure 36.2

	G	H	I	J	K	L	M	N	O	P	Q
1			2	3	4	5		Ln(Value)	-0.00623		
2	Allocation		0.111121	0.010242	0.878638			Value end of Year 1 (today's $s)	0.993789	Mean = .0748	
3	Beginning cash	Scenario	Bills	Bonds	Stocks	Inflation	Ending cash	Deflation			
4	1	1960	2.66	13.78	0.47	1.48	1.008496707	0.985415845			
5											
6								growth rate/yr	0.077669		

Step 1: In I2:K2 enter trial allocations of assets to T-Bills, bonds and stocks. Make sure they add up to 100%.

Step 2: In G4 enter Amanda's beginning Year 1 cash (1).

Step 3: In H4 we randomly choose a year as a scenario. To do this enter the formula

=RiskDuniform($A$4:$A$72)

in H4.

Step 4: In I4:L4 we "lookup" for each year the return on each asset and inflation rate corresponding to the chosen scenario. Note that our approach preserves historic correlations between asset returns and inflation. In I4 look up T-bill return with the formula

=VLOOKUP($H4,Lookup,I$1).

Using the scenario chosen in H4, this formula looks in column 2 of the lookup range to find T-bill returns. Copying this formula to I4:L4 generates asset returns and inflation.

Step 5: In cell M4 we compute the ending Year 1 value of Amanda's assets in with the formula

=G4($I$2*(1+(I4/100))+$J$2*(1+(J4/100))+$K$2*(1+(K4/100))).*

This formula takes the amount of money invested in each asset at the beginning of the year and changes its value based on the asset's return during the year.

Step 6: In N4 we compute the value (in today's dollars) of a dollar received at end of the year with the formula

=1/(1+(L4/100)).

Step 7: In cell O2 we compute, in today's dollars, the value of Amanda's portfolio at the end of a year.

*=M4*N4.*

Step 8: In O1 we compute the logarithm of the ending value (in today's dollars) of Amanda's assets with the formula

=LN(O2).

Step 9: We are now ready to use RISKOptimizer to determine the asset allocation which will (by Kelley criteria) maximize Amanda's expected long-run growth rate of her assets. Our Model window follows:

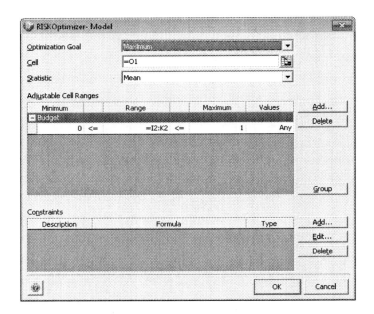

We choose to maximize the expected value of the logarithm of our final asset position (in today's dollars) (this is cell O1). Our adjustable cells are the asset allocations in cells I2:K2. We select the budget method to ensure that 100% of our capital is allocated. Constraining the asset proportions to be between 0 and 1 rules out short selling. RISKOptimizer finds that placing 11% in T-bills, 1% in bonds, and 88% in stocks optimizes long-term mean growth. Thus we again see (as we did in Chapter 22) the superiority of stocks for the long run. The average long-term annual growth rate (in real dollars) of our investments will be $e^{.0748} - 1 = 7.8\%$.

Reference

Kelly, J. "A New Interpretation of Information Rate," *Bell System Technical Journal*, Volume 35, pages 917-926.

Chapter 37: Optimal Selection of Employees

Hiring the best employees is crucial to an organization's success. Most hiring is based on a combination of interview and test results. Those who interview and test the best are hired. The key question is how good a score on interviewing and testing should be required before an prospective employee is hired. Employees who score better will presumably generate more profit for the company. The problem is that it is costly to interview forever and if we are too selective we may go bankrupt before hiring anybody! The following example shows how to use RISKOptimizer to determine optimal selection procedures.

Example 37.1   Eli Daisy needs to hire 5 people each year for its sales force. In evaluating prospective employees, Eli Daisy combines interviews and personality tests to give each prospective employee a score between 0 and 100. These scores appear to be normally distributed. Eli Daisy has tracked the annual sales revenue (in thousands of dollars) generated by past employees. See Figure 37.1 and file hr.xls.

Figure 37.1

	B	C
1	Score	Sales
2	33	10
3	50	697
4	78	735
5	85	695
6	42	167
7	53	416
8	62	448
9	58	444

For example, one employee scored 33 on the selection process and sold $10,000 worth of drugs per year, etc. Eli Daisy assumes that each employee stays with the company five years. A 10% profit is earned on each dollar of sales revenue and profits are discounted at 10% per year. Eli Daisy needs to hire five employees per year and it costs $1000 to screen a prospective applicant. What score on the screening exam should Lilly require for a new hire?

We begin by determining the distribution of scores on the screening exam. Next we determine the validity of the screening test. That is, how effective is the screening test in predicting sales revenue generated by the employee. Finally, we simulate a random stream of applicants and use RISKOptimizer to determine an optimal cutoff. See Figures 37.2-37.4 and file hr.xls.

Figure 37. 2

	D	E	F	G	H	I	J	K
1								
2				Sales	Stdev=214			
3	Score			Mean=55.03+8.97*Score				
4	Mean	60.92708		SUMMARY OUTPUT				
5	Sigma	14.25796						
6				Regression Statistics				
7				Multiple R	0.515083			
8				R Square	0.26531			
9				Adjusted R Square	0.257494			
10				Standard Error	214.037			
11				Observations	96			
12								
13				ANOVA				
14					df	SS	MS	F
15				Regression	1	1555088	1555088	33.94513
16				Residual	94	4306312	45811.82	
17				Total	95	5861400		
18								
19					Coefficients	Standard Error	t Stat	P-value
20				Intercept	55.02516	96.34744	0.571112	0.569287
21				X Variable 1	8.973429	1.540174	5.826245	7.9E-08
22								

Step by Step

Step 1: In cell E4 and E5 of sheet data we determine the mean and standard deviation of interview scores with the formulas (in E4)

$=AVERAGE(B2:B97)$

and (in E5)

$=STDEV(B2:B97).$

We can now model each prospective hire's score as a normal random variable with mean 60.93 and standard deviation 14.26.

Step 2: We now run a regression to predict annual sales revenue (in '000's) from test score. From Figure 37.2 the p-value of .00000008 shows that the test score is a significant factor in predicting sales. We therefore model the annual sales revenue (in '000's) generated by a prospective hire as a normal random variable with mean 55.03+ 8.97*score and standard deviation (equal to standard error of regression) of 214.04.

Step 3: In sheet model we now model the selection process. See Figure 37.3. In D1:I1 we enter relevant parameters. E1 contains a trial "cutoff value".

Figure 37.3

	B	C	D	E	F	G	H	I	J	K
1			Cutoff	81	Hire cost	1000	Profit	0.1		
2	Person	Hired to date	Score	Accept	Sales	Profit-Cost	Total hired	Total Profit	1330079	
3	1	0	72.72374	No	0	-1000	0			
4	2	0	84.01885	Yes	690.9305	260917	1			
5	3	1	47.3147	No	0	-1000	1			
6	4	1	54.39587	No	0	-1000	1		Mean =	
7	5	1	43.49847	No	0	-1000	1		1531164.9285	
8	6	1	90.12554	Yes	1077.927	407619	2			
9	7	2	65.03041	No	0	-1000	2			
10	8	2	66.58261	No	0	-1000	2			
11	9	2	54.4922	No	0	-1000	2			

Step 4: We will assume that interviewing 200 people should yield our five people (given the selection rule chosen by RISKOptimizer, this turns out to be the case). In C3 we compute the number of people hired so far: 0.

Step 5: In D3 we compute the score of the first person interviewed. We use the normal distribution estimated in Step 1.

=RiskNormal(60.93,14.25).

Step 6: In E3 we ensure the person is accepted if and only if their test score meets our cutoff.

=IF(D3>=$E$1,"Yes","No").

Step 7: In F3 we use our regression results to model the interviewee's sales productivity (based on her test score).

=IF(E3="Yes",RiskNormal(55.03+8.97*model!D3,214.04),0).

Note that if the person is not accepted they generate $0 sales. Otherwise the annual sales in ($000's) is normal with a mean equal to 55.03 + 8.97*(score) and standard deviation 214.04.

Step 8: In G3 we compute the profit contributed by this interviewee. If five people have already been hired, the current interviewee generates 0 profit, because we will have stopped the selection process. Otherwise, we include the $1000 cost of interviewing and the present value of profit generated by the employee's five years of sales. *Note that with the following syntax the Excel PV function can be used to generate the present value (assuming end of year payments) of $1 received for n years discounted at rate r.*

$$=-PV(r, n, 1).$$

We need the negative sign because the PV function returns a negative value. The following formula in G3 generates the profit contributed by the current interviewee.

$$=IF(C3<5,-\$G\$1,0)+IF(C3<5,\$I\$1*(-PV(0.1,5,1))*1000*F3,0).$$

Note that $I1*1000*F3$ is the employee's annual contribution to sales.

Step 8: In H3 we compute the total number hired to date by adding the current person (if hired) to previous hires.

$$=C3+IF(E3="yes",1,0).$$

Step 9: In C4 we compute number hired before second person is interviewed with formula

$$=H3.$$

Step 10: We now copy the formulas from D3:H3 to D4:H4. This generates the progress of interviewee 2. Copying the formulas D4:H4 to D5:H202 (after selecting D4:H4 double click on the cursor in lower right-hand corner of H4!) we have generated the progress of 200 potential interviewees.

Step 11: In cell J2 we compute total profit with the formula

$$=SUM(G3:G202).$$

Step 12: We are now ready to use RISKOptimizer to determine the cutoff point for selection that maximizes expected profit. Our Model window is as follows:

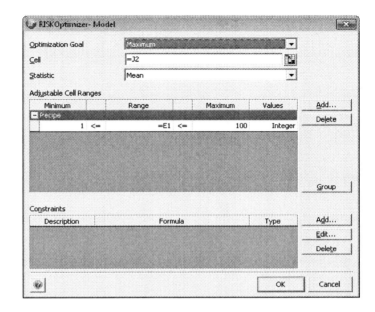

Our goal is to maximize our mean profit (cell J2) from hiring five employees by adjusting the cutoff point for selection (cell E1). RISKOptimizer reports that we can generate $1,531,164 by accepting all employees who score at least 81 on the selection process. Using the Excel NORMDIST function as follows we find that the optimal selection policy is to accept the top 8% of all applicants. To obtain the percentage accepted simply enter (see Figure 37.4)

=1-NORMDIST(81,60.93,14.25,1).

The "1" in NORMDIST ensures that Excel computes the cumulative normal probability rather than the normal density.

Figure 37.4

	I	J
11		Accepted
12		0.079503

Chapter 38: Using Exponential Smoothing for Quality Control

Many manufacturing firms produce products that are considered defective if a given measurement exceeds an Upper Specification Limit (USL) or is less than a Lower Specification Limit (LSL). Usually the measurement of the product depends on a machine setting, such as the mean measurement of products produced by the machine. In reality, the mean measurement produced by the machine drifts or changes through time and the manufacturer must decide when to reset the machine. The only information the manufacturer has is measurements of units produced since the last machine resetting. A reasonable strategy is to look at a weighted average of all measurements since the last resetting. If the weighted average is too high or too low reset the machine. Otherwise leave the machine alone. RISKOptimizer can be used to determine a policy of this type that minimizes expected cost per item. The following example illustrates the basic ideas.

Example 38.1 Jumpco produces elevator rails. Suppose an elevator rail is acceptable if and only if its diameter is between .999 and 1.001 inches. After being reset the machine that produces the rails produces elevator rails with a mean diameter of 1". After producing an elevator rail, the mean diameter of the rails produced changes according to a normal random variable with mean 0 and standard deviation .0004". The diameter of each elevator rail has a standard deviation of .0003" about the mean. A defective rail costs $250 while it costs $500 to reset the machine to a mean of 1". The question is under what circumstances should the machine be reset. We will adopt the following policy. Compute weighted average of all rails produced since last resetting as follows:

$$\text{New Weighted Average} = \lambda*(\text{current weighted average}) + (1 - \lambda)* \qquad \textbf{(38.1)}$$
$$(\text{current rail's diameter}).$$

λ must be between 0 and 1. Values of λ near zero give a lot of value to recent rails, while values of λ near one give little value to recently produced rails. After a reset, we initialize the weighted average to 1". We will reset the machine if the weighted average goes above an Upper cutoff C(1) or below a Lower cutoff C(2). Our goal is to use RISKOptimizer to determine values of C(1), C(2), and λ that minimize average cost per item produced.

We will simulate 200 items and try to minimize expected cost per item produced. Our work is in Figure 38.1 and file feedback.xls.

Figure 38.1

	A	B	C	D	E	F	G	H	I
1			Adjustme nt cost	500	item sigma	0.0003			
2			Defective cost	250	Lambda	0.777979			
3			LSL	0.999	Upper cut	1.0005			
4	Feedback		USL	1.001	Lower cut	0.9995			
5			drift sigma	0.0004			Cost/item	73.75	
6	Item #	Mean	Actual	Weighted Mean	Replace?	Cost			
7	1	1	1.000585	1	No	ͻ			
8	2	1.000123	1.000218	1.00013	No	ͻ			
9	3	1.000466	1.000595	1.000149	No	ͻ			
10	4	1.000948	1.000794	1.000248	No	ͻ		Mean = 85.7	
11	5	1.001673	1.001971	1.000369	No	250			
12	6	1.001779	1.00173	1.000725	Yes	750			
13	7	1	1.000067	1	No	ͻ			
14	8	1.000213	1.000459	1.000015	No	ͻ			
15	9	1.000686	1.000688	1.000114	No	ͻ			

Step 1: In C1:F4 we enter problem parameters including trial values of λ, C(1) (Upper cutoff) and C(2) (Lower cutoff).

Step 2: In cell B7 we enter the current mean for the machine (1").

Step 3: In cell C7 compute the actual diameter of the first rail with the formula

$=RiskNormal(B7,\$F\$1).$

We assume that rail diameters follow a normal distribution.

Step 4: In cell D7 initialize the weighted average diameter by entering a "1".

Step 5: In cell E7 we determine if current weighted average exceeds C(1) or is less than C(2). If so, we reset the current machine.

$=IF(OR(D7>\$F\$3,D7<\$F\$4),"Yes","No").$

Step 6: In cell F7 we compute the cost associated with the current item. This is the sum of the defective cost (if item is defective) and reset cost (if machine is reset).

$=IF(OR(C7>\$D\$4,C7<\$D\$3),\$D\$2,0)+IF(E7="yes",\$D\$1,0).$

Step 7: In cell B8 we compute mean for machine for second item. If machine is reset, mean equals 1". Otherwise mean drifts with a standard deviation of .0004".

=IF(E7="Yes",1,RiskNormal(B7,$D$5)).

Step 8: In cell C8 copy the formula from C7 to generate the diameter of the second item.

Step 9: In cell D8 update the weighted average after the second rail is observed with the formula

=IF(E7="Yes",1,$F$2*D7+(1-$F$2)*C7).

If machine is reset, weighted average is set to 1". Otherwise, we update weighted average using (38.1).

Step 10: We determine if machine is reset after second item is observed and cost of second item by copying the formula in E7:F7 to E8:F8.

Step 11: Select cells B8:F8 and double click on cross to copy these formulas to the range B9:F206. This generates the history of 200 elevator rails.

Step 12: In cell H5 compute average cost per item with the formula

=AVERAGE(F7:F206).

Step 13: We are now ready to use RISKOptimizer to determine the reset policy that minimizes mean cost per item. Our Model window is as follows:

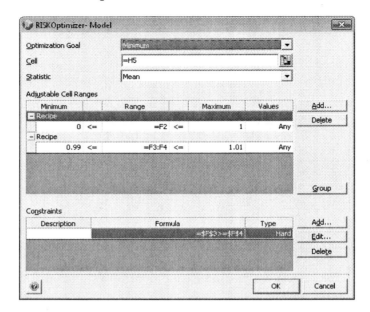

We choose to minimize mean average cost (cell H5) by adjusting λ (cell F2) and our Upper and Lower cutoffs (cells F3 and F4). We constrain λ to be between 0 and 1 and constrain our cutoffs to be between .99" and 1.01" For each simulation we constrain F3>=F4. This ensures our Upper cutoff is not smaller than our lower cutoff. RISKOptimizer uses λ= .77, an Upper cutoff of 1.005" and a Lower cutoff of .995". This strategy leads to a mean cost per item of $85.7.

Chapter 39: Bidding and the Winner's Curse

Consider an oil company that bids for the rights to drill in offshore areas. The value of the right to drill in a given offshore area is highly uncertain, as are the bids of the competitors. RISKOptimizer can be used to model bidding in such highly uncertain environments. Our example will demonstrate the **winner's curse**. The winner's curse states that the optimal bidding strategy entails bidding a substantial amount below your assumed value for the product you are bidding for. The idea is that if you do not bid under your assumed value, your uncertainty about the actual value of the product will often lead you to win bids for products on which you (after paying your high bid) lose money. The following example demonstrates the winner's curse and uses RISKOptimizer to model the bidding process.

Example 39.1   Royal Conch Oil is trying to determine a profit-maximizing bid for the right to drill on an offshore oil site. The value of the right to drill is unknown, but is equally likely to be any value between $10 million and $110 million. It is certain that between one and seven competitors will bid against us. The number of companies bidding against us is presently unknown, but when we bid we will know the number of bidders. Each bidder's (including us) estimate of the value of the drilling rights is equally likely to assume any number between 50% and 150% of the **actual value**. Based on past history, we believe that each competitor is equally likely to bid between 40% and 60% of their value estimate. Given this information, what fraction of our estimate should we bid in order to maximize our expected profit?

Solution   We will first solve the problem with seven competitors. Then it will be easy to solve the problem for less than seven competitors. Our work is in Figure 39.2 (see file winner.xls).

Figure 39.2

	A	B	C	D
1	**Winner's curse**			
2	Number of comp	7		
3	Fraction of estimate bid by us	0.663593		
4	True value	45.35867		
5	Our estimate	41.119		
6	Our bid	27.28628		
7	**Comp Estimates**			
8	Firm 1	33.24793		
9	Firm 2	58.46618		
10	Firm 3	49.41892		
11	Firm 4	22.85448		
12	Firm 5	37.55389		
13	Firm 6	41.456		
14	Firm 7	47.81932		
15	**Comp Bids**			
16	Firm 1	14.76424		
17	Firm 2	31.46676		
18	Firm 3	21.04969		
19	Firm 4	10.14144		
20	Firm 5	17.47057		
21	Firm 6	20.49304		
22	Firm 7	22.80638		
23	Do we win?	no		
24	Profit	0		
25				
26				
27				
28				Mean = 3.9772

Step by Step

Step 1: In cell B3 we enter a trial fraction of our estimate that we will bid.

Step 2: In B4 we generate the actual value of the lease with the formula

=RiskUniform(10,110).

Step 3: In B5 we generate our estimate of the actual value (noting we may be off by as much as 50%) with the formula

=RiskUniform(0.5*B4,1.5*B4).

Step 4: In B6 we compute our bid by multiplying our value estimate times the fraction of estimate that we bid.

=B3*B5.

Step 5: In B8:B14 we generate each competitor's estimate of the value by copying from B8 to B9:B14 the formula

=*RiskUniform(0.5*$B$4,1.5*$B$4)*.

Step 6: In B16:B22 we generate each competitor's bid as between 40% and 60% of the competitor's estimate of actual value by copying from B16 to B17:B22 the formula

=*RiskUniform(0.4*B8,0.6*B8)*.

Step 7: If our bid exceeds all other bids we win the bid. Otherwise we do not. This fact is denoted in B23 with the formula

=*IF(B6>=MAX(B16:B22),"yes","no")*.

Step 8: In B24 we compute the profit from our bid. If we win the bid we earn actual value - bid; otherwise we earn nothing.

=*IF(B23="yes",B4-B6,0)*.

Step 9: We are now ready to use RISKOptimizer to determine bid (as a fraction of our estimate) which maximizes our expected profit. Our Model window follows:

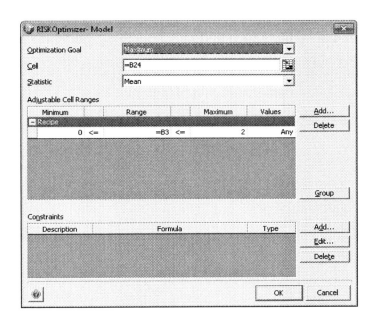

We choose to maximize mean profit (cell B24) by changing the fraction of our estimate (cell B3) bid. We constrain the bid (as fraction of estimate) to be between 0 and 2. RISKOptimizer indicates a maximum mean profit of $3.98 million. We should bid around 66% of our estimate of the site's value.

Remarks

If we want to find optimal bid fraction for six competitors, place a 0 in B16 and rerun the model. If we want to find the optimal bid fraction for five competitors, place a 0 in B16 and B17 and rerun the model, etc. You will find the optimal bid fractions and mean profit for each number of competitors to be (approximately) as follows:

# of Competitors	Mean profit per bid opportunity(millions)	Optimal Fraction of Estimate to Bid
7	$3.98	.66
6	$4.27	.66
5	$5.01	.65
4	$6.02	.64
3	$7.20	.62
2	$8.79	.62
1	$12.42	.60

We see that (consistent with the winner's curse), no matter how many competitors, our optimal bid is much less than our estimate of the site's value. Also each additional competitor reduces (at a decreasing rate) our mean profit. Also note that in the current example the number of competitors has little influence on our bidding strategy.

Index